Something
Nasty
in the
Slushpile

Something Nasty in the Slushpile

How *Not* To Get Published

Sammy Looker

Constable • London

CONSTABLE

First published in the UK by Constable,
an imprint of Constable & Robinson Ltd, 2014

A CIP catalogue record for this book
is available from the British Library.

ISBN: 978-1-47211-102-9 (hardback)
ISBN: 978-1-47211-107-4 (ebook)

Printed and bound by CPI Group (UK) Ltd, Croydon, CR0 4YY

Constable is an imprint of
Constable & Robinson Ltd
100 Victoria Embankment
London EC4Y 0DY

An Hachette UK Company
www.hachette.co.uk

www.constablerobinson.com

1 3 5 7 9 10 8 6 4 2

Dear Reader

This is a book for everyone – given that essentially we're all the same . . .

A big THANK YOU to everyone who has been involved
in this book. To Duncan Proudfoot, who came up with the
title and encouraged me on. To my editor, Hugh Barker,
who picked up the ball and ran the extra mile with it; who
did so much to help craft it. To The Brothers McLeod, who
captured the spirit of it and enhanced it with their enchanting
illustrations. To Chelsey Fox, who did what the best agents
do. To GN, for his support and creative input, particularly
the A–Z; for being there. To publisher Nick Robinson, 'an
unsnobbish gentleman . . . who preferred not to fish in the
main river', now gone but whose spirit of fine publishing lives
on. To the pluckiness and determination of aspiring authors,
who inspired, shocked and entertained in equal measure.

slush: partly melted watery snow; liquid mud, mire; excessively sentimental language, literature, etc. *Slush* or *slosh*, liquid mud, probably of Scandinavian origin, as in the Swedish *slask*, meaning wetness, liquid filth, and *slaska*, to paddle or wallow

Not to be confused with *slurry* or *sloshed* or *slush fund*

Akin to *sludge*, *mire*, *ooze* and *slutch*

pile: a heap of things of considerable height, laid or lying on one another [Old & modern French for heap, pyramid, mass of masonry, from the Latin *pila* for pillar, pier, mole]

Not to be confused with pile, as in a dart or arrow or a heavy javelin carried by a Roman foot soldier. Nor down nor hair. Nor haemorrhoid (usually plural)

Akin to pile as small castle or tower

slushpile or ***slush pile***: the term for the accumulated stack of unsolicited manuscripts sent to a publishing house with a view to publication. Note unsolicited, as in unsought, as in uninvited, dispatched by aspiring authors unrepresented by a literary agent, who would otherwise match author to publisher

origins the resemblance of a pile of typescripts, all black ink and white paper, to slushy snow. Or perhaps a nod to the leftover nature of unsolicited work – not part of the mainstream publishing event, left to melt and vanish without trace

purpose to discover and publish previously unpublished voices

Who'd Be
a Slushpile
Reader?

Sammy Looker was Constable's long-serving slushpile reader. He joined the firm in 1923 and was still there four decades later. Looker by name, Looker by nature; with a name like that, he had to be searching for something, and in his case it was authors.

It was Looker's job, and the ongoing task of those who succeeded him, to read and assess the unpublished work that arrived each week, to report favourably on anything that showed promise or otherwise recommend rejection. Looker's colleagues knew when he had passed them a manuscript to consider as some of the pages would be stuck together with the fishpaste from the sandwiches that he liked to eat while reading.

Slushpile reading was, and remains, a job akin to panning for gold. You might spend years knee-deep in earth or mud, caked in it up to your armpits; panning, sifting, squatting in a flowing river; finding nothing, until one day Bingo! Mining records from the days of the California gold rush describe finds on land so rich that sometimes gold in excess of £50,000 might be sifted from a single pan. Wealth like that, whether in gold prospecting or book publishing, is rare – as Pulitzer Prize-winning author James Michener recalled from his own personal experience.

Michener had at one time worked as a slushpile reader, a role he later talked about during an interview with author and New Journalist Tom Wolfe. When Wolfe asked Michener if he had ever worried about the competition from up-and-coming writers buried deep within the slushpile, Michener replied that if Wolfe had ever read a slushpile he would know that there was little to worry about.

Michener's view might sound jaundiced, but most slushpile readers start off jaunty and full of optimism, hopeful of striking publishing gold. But, at some stage, there is a rude awakening – with submissions that just don't fit a publisher's list, genres that individual firms don't publish (a fact easily established before sending); topics too esoteric and non-commercial; proposals overly academic for a trade publisher with a commercial readership and vice versa; submissions that are well written but poorly targeted; good ideas but badly executed; the quite off beam or simply preposterous. So the time has come for a ruminative rummage through the slushpile, to sample its wonders and its weirdness, its comedy, its tragedy and all points in between.

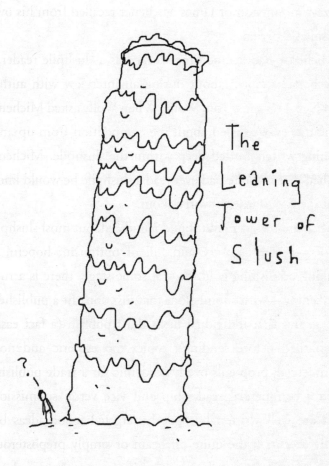

The Leaning Tower of Slush

Part 1

An idea's formed, the imagination engaged, research done, midnight oil burnt and book written (or at least a synopsis). Thereafter the next step on the publishing journey might be an exploratory enquiry, some preliminary research via writers' handbooks, bookshops or online, to establish a suitable publisher and their preferred submission procedure; then followed by a carefully tailored letter to introduce oneself and one's work. This is the perfect opportunity to present oneself and one's treasure in an ideal light, to tempt the publisher to take things further – but sometimes the best-laid plans can go awry . . .

Dear Reader

Let's get straight to the point – I am sitting here, in a garden shed, of all places . . .

The main character in the novel I've sent you is an impoverished wastrel – which makes him unfortunately similar to yours truly. But you can help me to take that first step away from the brink of the void.

I anticipate your swift response and look forward to working with you.

Yours sincerely

I am working on a project about the migration of fruit and vegetables across the globe throughout history, and, at the same time, on the endearing story of a transatlantic hot-air balloon race for mice and other rodents and on the travails of an appealing, accident-prone mongoose and extra ferret-y adventures.

So that I can allocate my time most efficiently, which one do you think you would want to publish first?

In the improbable circumstances that your interest might be piqued by my account of a bucolic village whose inhabitants include an embezzling vicar, a lady novelist of a certain age and a gin-soaked elf, I should be pleased to let you see more.

For many years I have been debating with myself whether to try to write. The idea filled me with longing but I lacked the self-belief to sit down and try. But, as with so many things in life, a tipping point can be reached where you wake up one day and say, My God, I really am going to give this a go . . .

A Mr Thompson gets in touch – he had been expecting contact about a submission he had e-mailed to the reader a week earlier and was impatient to hear back. Would someone give him a call, please? The receptionist jots down his phone number, followed by a password, something like Flymister (she didn't quite catch it), the name of a Cliff Richard film (she thinks, although she might well have misheard him). A password? Mr Thompson explains he has been receiving death threats and will only respond to callers who use it.

Dear Sir or Madam

Nothing is as it first seems . . .

I am enclosing some chapters of one of my tales for your perusal. The various storylines make it a story within a story with further layers of narrative curling ever inwards like a nautilus shell. I would be honoured if you would allow me to bestow a new ambience on your corporation.

Dear Sirs

One legitimate question that might be asked is what makes me want to write creatively in the first place?

Firstly let me say that I have no interest in either fortune or fame. However, I have an understanding of the temptations of vanity, and I will admit that seeing my name in a bookshop or library would bring a quiet sense of satisfaction.

But the truth is I simply feel compelled to write. I don't know if it is fate, the spirits or simple vocation but I have a strong urge to put pen to paper and to have my story published.

Your assistance would be greatly appreciated.

Yours faithfully

Dear Madam

In the hope that I might distract you from the hamster wheel of human existence, I have something to show you that is guaranteed to make your ears prick and your eyes bulge.

I am submitting a proposal for the book *Dog Tails: Paws for Thought*. Animal stories are perennially popular, and this one has every element of a bestseller in the making. It includes tales of life-saving dogs, rescue dogs, cartoon dogs. Plus a few shaggy-dog stories to boot.

Of the various readers who've finished my little book so far, all say there have been no unpleasant side-effects or troubling contra-indications.

Celebrity cookbooks are all the rage. Unfortunately I am not a celebrity, indeed most people on my own street would not be able to tell you my name. But I think it's about time that someone distinctively anonymous like me brought out a new recipe book for all the other interested unknowns out there.

There are many like me, who love eating and cooking. And my approach is unique and aimed at them. It's brimming with budget meals that are easy to rustle up from everyday store-cupboard ingredients. Even so, the dishes themselves aren't cheap, just inventive and imaginative. I'm an audacious cook, and the book will reflect that. I am enclosing a taster range of a week's recipes. Day 1: Spag Bol Soup, featuring Spag Bol flavours (Italian food, yum!), Sandy Bay Tuna (one of my all time favourite seaside resorts & it's fine to use tinned tuna), plus, to finish, a clever, satisfying little pud, Rhubarb Pie with Eton Mess.

Lord of the Rungs: A Book of Ladders is what it says it is; intended as both a DIY handbook and a tribute to an unsung hero of the everyday.

Where would we be without our ladders?

With tips on buying, using and storing garden ladders, domestic step ladders, easy-stow loft ladders, extension ladders, platform step ladders, telescopic ladders, trestle ladders, step stools, window-cleaning and fire-escape ladders, hedge-cutting tripod ladders – in aluminium or wood. Includes safety tips.

Plus a look at the more esoteric Christmas Tree ladders, cat ladders, pompier ladders, orchard and turntable ladders as well as ceremonial ladders, like the Javanese sugar-cane ladders of Indonesia, used symbolically in a life-affirming ritual to indicate confidence and determination in life.

And when it's time to replace it, you can always recycle your old ladder, giving it a brand-new lease of life as a bedside table, a bedroom-storage hanging rack for your clothes, shoes and accessories, a kitchen stand, a towel rail in the bathroom, a bookshelf, perhaps hung horizontally, in the living room or for wall storage, an airing rack in the laundry room. If you're really inventive you could even transform it into a decorative piece, a stylish sculpture for your home or garden; wire it up as a ladder light, for wall or ceiling; use it as signage, for example, wrapping it in knitting squares if you run a wool shop or decorating it with flowers for a florists. All this and more. We show you how to make the most of your ladder in a book with wide appeal, both practical and aesthetic.

As they say, the ladder of success is best climbed via the rungs of opportunity.

How did I ever manage without my cat ladder?

Modames

The laptop witch preparng this work had some qwerks I did not sea due ov my not pacient person and hurry. Any big errors are not conseqwnt bad noledge inglish but computer and speed – planely.

~~~ 📎 ~~~

Some people wonder how they would cope if their book became a runaway bestseller. If there did happen to be a pot of gold at the end of that particular rainbow, I believe that I would have the wit and experience to handle it.

~~~ 📎 ~~~

My *Flavours of the Globe* is a collection of the many and varied recipes I have developed through experimentation and guesswork in the kitchen and on the barbecue. It will be fun and stylish with a dreamy delightful feel to it – fully illustrated with fabulous colour photographs not just of each dish but also of the exact spot in which the inspiration for the dish first came to me, whether it be a beachfront taverna in Old Naxos Town, or the wonderful Flower Forest in Barbados . . .

A business proposal, You Can Do It: How to Build Your Dream, arrives as a finished book, bound in blue loop-pile carpet, a square left over, perhaps, from carpeting the sender's bathroom, possibly a nod to blue-sky thinking or just the colour of a favourite football team.

A worthy successor in the Darling-you-shouldn't-have-gone-to-so-much-trouble stakes arrives a week later, wrapped in bright-green AstroTurf, although this is a sports-book proposal, something along the lines of my life as a cricket fan.

Note to self: you can't judge a book by its cover.

Us book lovers are desperate for something different, something fresh. I think my moment's come, and I would want you to push my work all over the world, on Kindle, in print, across the whole fandango . . .

Something Nasty in the Slushpile

I'm hot!

LIFE of PIE

I am sending you the first in a proposed new series, provisionally called *Life of Pies*.

Life of Apple Pie. Featuring recipes and a social and cultural look at one of the world's favourite pies. From English Bramley Pie to French tarte Tatin, German Apfelkuchen, Greek Milopita, Italian Crostata di mele and American Hot Apple Pie, this is one popular fruit pie. In the US there is even a National Apple Pie Day every May, which just about pips everyone to the post: the nation that ate all the apple pies.

Market: For anyone who likes pies – and everyone likes pies.

More in the *Life of Pies* series:

Life of American Pies: US's National Pie Day is 23 January and America has a big pie history and some great pies, including Shoofly Pie and Mississippi Mud Pie, Hoosier Sugar Cream Pie, French Silk Pie (quintessentially American and runner-up in the 1951 Pillsbury Bake-Off), Key Lime Pie and many, many more.

Europe's Pie Chart: from German Zwiebelkuchen (Onion Pie), Amish Sauerkraut Surprise Custard Pie and Black Forest Cream Pie to Greek Galatopita or Milk Pie and Portokalopita or Sweet Orange Pie.

And crossover pies featuring such classics as Tourtière, the French–Canadian Meat Pie. In preparation: Cream Pies; Tasty Tarts; Meaty Pies; Humble Pies.

Hiya

There is most certainly a desire to read more ghost stories of a supernatural nature. And my story is unique. It is a spook romance, featuring a dazzling beautiful boy, who journeys into death on the back of his madness, and an apocryphal beast, a shape-shifting Xanthus, an immortal horse with the power of speech.

But beyond its central story of beauty and the beast, it also involves a spiritual journey and life in faraway lands, inviting us to question the core of our existence: where we have come from and why we are here.

My grandson is in the middle of his gap year . . . Would you like to publish his e-mails? Everyone who's read them says they are riveting.

Nearly every single living, breathing person in the world will want to read this book!

I wonder if you would consider my story of Marilyn M and how & why she died? I am now in the evening of my life and before I go I would like for other people to know of what actually occurred. There are many, many books on MM, and people never tire of her or of her story. I thought that you might find my thoughts on the events and the reasons enlightening – and of interest to a wider public.

Respectfully

Since you last rejected it, I have totally re-written my novel about the years I lived in the Congo. However, it is not yet ready, so I am submitting some sample pages of several entirely new works and include summaries of them all for your consideration, among them and including *Tick-a-Tock-a-Tack!: The Relentless Clock and How to Stop It*, and *Basic Budget Breakfasts for One*, or *A Small Cook Book for Mini Meals on a Primus* OR *Why Don't You Just Slap a Lid On It*.

'P' for Pass,
'R' for Reject

Conventional wisdom has it that just 10 per cent of the slushpile is of interest (although not necessarily publishable). The rest can be dispatched whence it came, without further ado. But surely not everyone is as organized as New York literary journal The Paris Review *when it comes to dealing with hopeful authors and their work.*

Founded in Paris in 1953, *The Paris Review* launched with its mission statement of welcoming and publishing 'good writers and good poets, the non-drumbeaters and non-axe-grinders. So long as they're good.'

The magazine still invites submissions (but not by e-mail and rejected manuscripts without return postage are neither replied to nor returned). Each submission is considered by at least two readers; if one likes it and the other doesn't, it is read by a third person. Anything with two 'Ps' for 'pass' (versus 'R' for 'reject') is then read by an editor. But despite its warm welcome, if the *Review* were to publish just one piece each year from the slushpile, as it reportedly has done, that means each submission has a slim .008 per cent chance of success.

One aspiring author who lucked out was Philip Roth. Unknown and barely published, Roth's short story 'The

Conversion of the Jews' was extracted from the *Review*'s submissions and published in 1959 as part of his debut, *Goodbye, Columbus, and Five Short Stories*. It won a National Book Award in 1960, a notable achievement for an anthology of short stories from a new author. A decade or so later, the title novella, *Goodbye, Columbus*, was adapted for Hollywood, subsequently winning a Writers Guild of America Award.

The Paris Review is known for its quality writing and talent-spotting credentials. According to its website, it was the first to publish T. Coraghessan Boyle, V. S. Naipaul, Adrienne Rich, Mona Simpson, Edward P. Jones and Rick Moody. Excerpts from Samuel Beckett's *Molloy* featured in an early issue, published in English. It was also an early advocate of Jack Kerouac, publishing his short story 'The Mexican Girl' in 1955 (which later appeared in part one of *On the Road*). Other contemporary literary landmarks that first graced its pages include Donald Barthelme's *Alice*, Italo Calvino's *Last Comes the Raven*, Jim Carroll's *Basketball Diaries*, Jeffrey Eugenides's *Virgin Suicides*, Jonathan Franzen's *The Corrections*, Peter Matthiessen's *Far Tortuga* – and, of course, Philip Roth's *Goodbye, Columbus*.

Sorry to Bother You . . .
Some First Lines

You never have a second chance to make a first impression. So how to stand out from the crowd? That covering letter, the one that introduces your publishing idea, must grab the reader's attention and highlight your proposal's unique potential. So how to maximize that initial impact?

Well, luck might find you seated next to a book-world mover and shaker one night at dinner or during a long train journey and feeling emboldened to seize the day. Or you may be a graduate from a high-profile creative-writing programme, such as the campus for novelists at the University of East Anglia, and you can flourish that as your calling card. Or you could choose to get yourself noticed by landing a helicopter outside the door of your chosen publisher with a banner declaring your intentions. Otherwise, here are a few ideas from the slushpile.

- There is a murderer on the loose. His target? Publishers . . .

- I'm about to be blunt now, so hang on to your hat.

- Abject apologies for disturbing you but . . .

- I propose to keep this just as terse, tight and to the point as I can.

- After numerous books of criticism, I have set my sights on a subject that only I can do justice to: the fully illustrated, full-colour, panoramic 3D history of me.

- I am a retired lawyer (specialising in wills and probate). Not, I appreciate, the most beguiling of introductions . . .

- Would you like to join me on my journey to hell and back?

- New to writing, I am quite unacquainted with its protocols, and the whole ghastly business of publishing, but, it goes without saying, I come with a tale to tell and a story to sell.

- I see no need to explain the content and purpose of what you are about to read – it would just make this e-mail much too long and complicated.

- I fervently hope that your current state is one of extravagant happiness and boundless joy.

- Please keep your eyes peeled for this little shocker.

- Hopefully, you will find enclosed a synopsis and the opening chapters of my novel (don't worry – they are all very brief & won't take a minute to consider).

- I am engaged in assembling the autobiography of my own life . . .

- I do so respect the outstanding success of your esteemed publishing company *[flattery will get you nowhere]*.

- I proudly hereby submit a powerpoint presentation of my first book.

- My story is unique . . .

- Please send your thoughts on my manuscript to me at Dauphin County (Prison Inmate No.797K) . . . Keep the fact in mind that I have been incarcerated here and elsewhere for a great many years.

- I do appreciate that you're immensely busy. I hope you won't find my writing to you a problem.

- I have just come to the end of writing a fictional novel.

- You'll be pleased to hear that I've calculated that in an average-sized paperback format, this book is made up of 57,691 words, 34 tables, 95 figures, front and back jacket, total 354 pages. It has not been published yet.

- I choose to write under a pseudonym, because I wouldn't want to reveal my true identity. The title under which I am writing this letter is not mine either. It is beyond vital that I remain anonymous.

- When I ran my idea for this book past an acquaintance of mine who edits documentaries for Channel 5 and other stations, she said it would definitely be a great success.

- This might be a silly question but . . .

- You are requested to view a significant submission for your perusal. In order to view this proposal, please click on the link below. The document has been uploaded using a secured file uploader. You will be required to sign in with your e-mail and to create a personalised password in order to view this highly confidential document *[and then say Abracadabra]*.

- We know from television programmes such as *Who Do You Think You Are?* that people are generally fascinated to learn as much as they are able about their ancestral & family history. I consider myself blessed to have been born into an especially enthralling one.

- I am now mulling over the possibility of permitting a publisher to put together a pioneering book based on my daily blog posts. Please be aware that I have approached several publishers simultaneously with this suggestion, so, to avoid missing out, do let me know by return if this would be something for you?

The Leaning Tower
of Slush

A publisher's slushpile can reach epic proportions. Left untended, it grows vast then tottery then leans, threateningly – at which point help might be drafted in to deal with it.

A few publishers still employ dedicated slushpile readers. However, they are a dying breed, as publishing houses increasingly refuse to accept unsolicited work and use other means to build their lists. Once upon a time, however, the majority of publishers employed manuscript readers (and, before postage costs soared and when staff levels permitted, were courteous enough, generally, to send a card acknowledging every submission they received). Many of them, like reader-turned-Pulitzer-Prize-winner James Michener, were immersed in the world of books and at work in all aspects of it to earn a living.

ROSE MACAULAY (later Dame Rose) became a reader for Constable following the death of the company's main reader, O'Grady, in the First World War. Her own first satirical book, *What Not*, was published by Constable at the end of the War, followed by *Three Days* in 1919. Her last novel, *The Towers of Trebizond*, has a memorable opening sentence involving a camel and High Mass. During the Second World War Macaulay lost everything, including her book collection, when her house was bombed during the Blitz.

In 1913, medieval scholar and translator HELEN WADDELL's debut, *Lyrics from the Chinese*, a collection of thirty-six poems, was published and became an instant success (in those days this could mean selling just 1000 copies over several months). However, in spite of her success, Waddell still needed to supplement her income (aspiring authors, please note: nothing much has changed). This she did by working as a manuscript reader for Constable, which, recognizing her own merits as an author, subsequently published her study of the *vagantes* of the Middle Ages, *The Wandering Scholars*. After Waddell became a full-time staff member, she went on to write three more books, including a novel and bestselling collection of children's stories.

Journalist and author of *Himglish and Femalese: Why Women Don't Get Why Men Don't Get Them*, JEAN HANNAH EDELSTEIN's first job post-uni was in publishing and included panning the slushpile for gold. As she described in a blog, 'The Shocking Truth about the Slushpile', she started out optimistically, confident that from deep within the heaps of unsolicited typescripts she would unearth buried treasure; believing herself 'some kind of beneficent tweedy sprite, conveying the writing of unknown literary artistes to the masses'. By the time she left the job, that belief was eroded, worn down by the book proposals she read that described a heart-felt wish 'to write full time … in a villa overlooking the Mediteranian, despite the fact that they didn't know how to spell it'.

ROSE STYRON, poet, journalist and wife of Pulitzer Prize-winning novelist William Styron, author of *Sophie's Choice*, was a reader for literary magazine *The Paris Review* in the 1950s. It was Styron who discovered Philip Roth in the *Review*'s slushpile.

Sometimes described as author–journalist Joan Didion's younger and more pugnacious sister, RENATA ADLER, a member of the American Academy of Arts and Letters, was the *New York Times'* first female film critic. Starting out as a manuscript reader for the *New Yorker* magazine, the long, intricate reports she wrote were entirely negative, having never come across anything as contemporary as she was required to read at the college from which she had recently graduated. None the less, the magazine went on to publish almost all the work, mostly from *New Yorker* stars, on which she had reported so negatively. Her poor strike record didn't impinge on her subsequent career either, with Adler becoming a *New Yorker* staff writer and the author of two modernist novels, *Speedboat* and *Pitch Dark*, the former awarded the Ernest Hemingway prize for best first novel in 1976.

When HEATHER GODWIN faced the Heinemann slushpile in the 1980s it was a looming Everest that overshadowed the editorial department. She reduced it to its foothills, although the mountain was ever in danger of re-forming as new submissions arrived daily. Her work was not in vain. From it she pulled Roddy Doyle's *The Commitments*, then self-published; later she extracted Bill Bryson's *The Lost Continent*. Her skill for spotting new writing talent was subsequently channelled into the London-based literary agency that she co-founded.

SAMANTHA SHANNON's debut novel, *Aurora*, was written but unpublished during the time she was employed as an agency reader. The many cover letters from aspiring authors that accompanied the submissions she read reminded her of the equally heartfelt ones that she had written in her attempt to get *Aurora* published.

As Shannon sifted through the slushpile, she wanted to find a voice that resonated or an idea that sparked her interest, but, when she did not, it dawned on her that her novel might have been similarly received. But her story has a happy ending, with a six-figure publishing deal for the fantasy-novel sequence that she wrote post-*Aurora*.

On her blog, 'A Book from the Beginning', Shannon says that *Aurora*'s rejection toughened her up, both personally and as a writer; acted as a stepping stone to her subsequent success. She launched the blog as a new writers' resource, describing her publication journey and life as a published writer, as well as other aspects of the publishing industry and literary world.

And a wannabe reader

In 2003, US writer JOHN WARNER, spurred on by an imminent change in fiction editor at the *New Yorker*, wrote an article encouraging the new editor to renew the magazine's long-term commitment to the slushpile as a source of unpublished gems. Disappointed at what he saw as the gradual disappearance of a potential lifebelt for under-published writers, and an ongoing description of slushpile authors as 'unsavvy' about the process of publishing and writing, he offered to read the *New Yorker*'s unsolicited submissions for a month to see what treasures he might find there. He also devised an elaborate public-voting system to process them. If none of this bore fruit, what is certain today is that the public has plenty of opportunity to comment and review ongoing and published work, on Amazon and elsewhere.

Part 2

Working initially in the US film business, as a reader or story analyst for a leading Hollywood literary agent, screenplay consultant, independent producer and teacher, Michael Hauge's brief was to find the one-in-a-hundred screenplays worth considering. At first he thought his new employers had got it wrong with such an under-estimation. By Hauge's own reckoning, at least half of all the scripts he might be asked to read would have some merit, but in any case, given that he was, as he puts it, 'just off the turnip truck from Oregon', he halved his guess-timate to accommodate what he saw as the agency's pessimism.

A week or so into his new job, Hauge took stock and realized he was wrong; that the agency had got it wrong too. Screenplays worthy of more than a glance proved to be as rare as hens' teeth. And so Hauge must have sensed an opportunity when he went on to write his bestselling book about how to write screenplays that sell.

Dear Sir or Madam

What is the meaning of life? My story answers that question from my viewpoint, but it will be of interest to others who want to discover how to make sense of things. Mine is an investigative account with many strands: romance, humour, horror, excitement, crime, fear, philosophy, spirituality, death. It also tackles purposelessness.

Your submission guidelines make it clear that I should include information on my previous experience. I have none worth a candle – except perhaps for publication on a few rare occasions, decades ago, in what are the now entirely obsolete underground magazines *IT* and *Oz*.

I developed a phobia about flying some years back. It meant I was restricted to holidays at home etc., which wasn't easy for me or the family. Then I discovered cognitive behavioural therapy (CBT) and the idea of distraction techniques. This has enabled me to feel the fear and do it anyway. Over the years, I've refined it, so that, after I get on board and settled in my seat, I start making little sketches of everyone sitting near by. Then I spend the rest of the flight writing captions to my drawings, inventing stories based on them.

I'd tried the usual tranquillizers and alcohol, but that only made me worse. This really works; I have been doing it for a while now and I have enough material for a decent-sized book. I'd like to call it *Air Shots*, and I believe it would sell well in airport bookstores and otherwise, generally, as a self-help book. I hope you share my enthusiasm.

I am sending you my first novel. It is a sad story with a sad ending. It will not be my last. That has an even sadder ending.

Good night

My name is José, I am Portuguese and living England.

I been in India, Goa, when I wrote the book – more than 200,000 words in under a quarter of a year. It did not require any struggle to write. It just came pouring out me, like always it was inside me and I just needed to open the right trapdoor to find it.

Back in Portugal an xpert in errars including the grammer, so that you will be happy see there are (perhaps little) no mistakes. I need your corporation to translate from Portuguese into English and then get publish by you selves, will, will, please, assist you me?

It is preparing to coming out with an online bokshupt publisherr.

Thank you very much.

Dear Submission Dept

Huge apologies for not sending this covering letter with my original submission last week. I had meant to include it, but I left in a rush for the post office and discovered it on my chair. I must have been sitting on it.

I have no knowledge or experience of mountain climbing or indeed ever walked much at all, in a recreational sense, at least. I am just a generally out of shape, regular guy with virtually no sense of direction or any survival training or skills. I aim to climb the world's highest mountain and write a book about it: *Everest for Dummies.*

I plan to raise the funds to do this from a book deal. I shall donate a portion of any proceeds to charity. I trust this is something that might interest you?

Dummy

Hi

This has to be brief because I have engineered an illicit window of opportunity to contact you, given that I was sectioned a few days ago and have (officially) no access to email, web or indeed much else . . . The fact is, I'm in a spot of bother right now, to put it mildly, and can't pop out to the mail box with this, so I hope you will accept an email proposal.

Sirs

Unseen, a breath-taking and multi-layered epic, is my first real attempt at publishing and in view of my advanced age possibly the last.

It is a work of fiction that uses anthropomorphism for characterization – with a political and religious edge to the novelization. Every character in the book is based on someone I know but of course I wouldn't tell them that.

If you would like to see some examples, please get in touch.

Gandhi drank his; J. D. Salinger was a fan; in China, millions drink a daily dose; it's even recommended in the Bible: Drink waters from thy own cistern, flowing water from thy own well.

My book is about the health benefits of drinking your own pee, known medically as auto-urine therapy. It will show that this is not just a way out of a tight spot, when dehydration threatens survival, but also a day-to-day tactic for achieving optimal health. With accompanying supportive documentation, my book will explain the many and various life-saving advantages of pee-drinking.

Furthermore, this is something everyone can do without any extra effort or expense, requiring no outlay and bringing unbounded rewards. And it's a topic that attracts strong views and is divisive and widely debated. There will be a lot of interest. And it will help a lot of people.

My suggested titles are *The Golden Fountain* or *Taking the Piss*.

Please find some cover ideas attached, too, so you'll have a clearer sense of where I'm going with this.

Cheers!

A shiny, black quilted Jiffy bag with a baby pink address label bears the instruction FRAGILE! I JUST NEED SOMEONE TO CARE. *Inside, swaddled in crêpe paper and cotton wool, is a tiny hand-crafted gift, a little doll encircled by poinsettias, with a speech-bubble label that reads: 'The hummingbirds have brought you this as a present.' An accompanying stamped addressed postcard of Lake Como is to be used to reply, should 'any great notions ever go ping in your marvellous mind'.*

Dear Editor

I am writing to you today to ask if you may like to publish my first fictional book? In my opinion it is a jolly good read . . .

At the risk of annoying, could I please invite your immediate response, given that an answer would be most welcome due to my imminent last posting.

WHEN YOU RESPOND TO ME, DO PLEASE HELP BY EMPLOYING A BOLD AND EXTRA LARGE FONT THAT ASSISTS THE SIGHT, NOW DIMMING.

MUCH OBLIGED

GREETINGS

The Happy Bunny Manifesto is a litmus test for good business acumen. The primary and potent reason for writing this book is for it to act as an aide-memoire, particularly on how to achieve success when I feel discouraged or reach the end of my tether in the workplace. It is my unique how-to succeed in business book.

At the heart of the Manifesto are four questions that I need to ask myself when necessary (in times of distraction or distress) to ensure the will for success (to live) returns. This gives me something fundamental and clear on which to focus, so I feel as if I am in charge and in complete control.

(A)   Are you a happy bunny? (Yes/No)

If your answer is yes, go no further! if no, move on to B:

(B)   Can you imagine being a happy bunny?
(C)   And how to become a happy bunny?
(D)   Then you know what you need to do next.

If this does not cheer you and lead you on to the path of joy, then repeat as necessary.

Dear Sir

I wanted to send you a novel but I live in the South Pacific and the postal service is just too erratic for me to trust, so I have decided to e-mail you instead. Please find the first few pages of my book . . . It is in total 400,000 words long and the first of a planned three-volume examination of the meaning of life. It deals with all the usual crap – and the highlights too.

Dear Publishers

I no longer dare to recall how blatantly bad the world smells. Its unholy stench seems inescapable. But I do regret the loss of the enduring trace and enticing aroma of tobacco; indeed, of cigarettes, cigars and pipes – before the health brigade banished them.

My book covers that most unfashionable and demonised of subjects, smoking, in all its permutations . . . from the first puff to the last, it carries on where Simon Gray & his smoking diaries left off.

On the Brink: Five Steps to Madness *arrives by courier. Every surface of the envelope records when and where it has been security checked, etc. It proves almost impossible to open, with the envelope wrapped in plastic and sealed with layers of brown duct tape. Inside, the spiral-ring-bound proposal is encased in a transparent yet sealed sleeve folder then wrapped in cardboard and sheets of tracing paper – unwrapping becoming a solitary game of pass the parcel.*

Out of another proposal envelope emerge five flimsy supermarket plastic bags, each tied in a triple knot by the handles, then all bound together by an elastic band. Cutting through the band and untying the knots takes some time, only to reveal a collaged cover letter and an agonized submission from an aspiring author who has seen trying times and whose work pivots on the question: Does the Devil exist?

More eye-catching and ever more inaccessible is what turns out to be a debut novel, parcelled up in its ring binder with an entire reel of red and white FRAGILE sticky tape.

Note to self: fragile authors approaching the brink?

Hello Hello Hello

How's tricks in Publishing Land?

Can I interest you in *Sole Witness*? It's a quirky murder mystery featuring Pete 'Sole' Parkinson, a brilliant private detective who also happens to be a foot fetishist. I have attached a summary of the plot and the first three chapters.

I believe there would be a strong commercial market for this book, both amongst lovers of quirky crime novels and the foot. In the States there's even an organization for those people, mostly men, who have a highly developed sexual interest in feet. In any event, podophilia (as it is known) is a frankly global phenomenon.

Foot fetishism, which is now not a designated perversion but a paraphilia or sexual partialism, plays a major role in Parkinson's ability to crack complex cases. In particular his encyclopedic knowledge of historic cases such as the Arkansas Toe Suck Fairy, who set up as a podiatrist in order to fondle feet; the French government minister who resigned over allegations that he had 'sexually molested' two of his female employees' feet.

Future titles would involve other puns, for instance *Sole Suspect, Sole Alibi, Sole Arrest, Sole Down the River* . . .

I have been looking for something to ground me and remind me that self-fulfilment is a goal for which I should strive; that in order to balance work and life successfully I need strategies for success. The previous problem I had was that I was on the trail of something that was not real until it was real. In order that I and others might understand this difficulty I pose one simple question – does it smell like fresh bread?

So when you have a new business idea, just ask yourself this single question.

Does it smell like fresh bread?

If so, you are on to a winner. If not, what more can you do to make it smell like fresh bread?

There has previously been a hugely successful business book about cheese entitled 'Who Moved My Cheese?' but I do not believe there are any comparable books on the market on the virtues of fresh bread, its value as an idea, an inspiration and an aim for daily life.

Me and My Beard

To beard or not to beard, that was the question when I wrote a blog about deciding to and then growing a beard – how long it took me, the different stages, from stubble to bushy, how I felt about it, days when I wanted to give up etc, what my friends thought, my girlfriend, reactions, good and bad, from my family and my mates.

I took daily photos of me on my beard journey and posted them on Facebook. I believe the blog and photos could be a fun book present and useful for anyone who fancies growing a beard, with beard tips and beard styles, from Henry VIII to Becks. The pros and the cons; the ups and the downs. What happened when I shaved it off – to me; to the blog; with my girlfriend.

I have an idea for a follow-up: *Me and My Hair*, a photo diary of when I decided to grow my hair long (and what happened when I had it all chopped).

Champagne, stylings, beech, rompings, diamonds, sex, romance . . . Everyone desire the celebrity lifestyle, like superstars today? Around each corner a new excitement and glamour places! The fashions, the models all complete crazy, but high entertaining and beyond. The characters are all good looks, like Albaro, his muscles rippling in white suit. His biggest opponent Joachim, another skydiver, Chilean. Bad, mad, dangerous, crazy. And his big rival, Vlad, chiselled cheeks, who is huge rock star in Russia. Rock shows, fashion campaigns, photograph shouts, trendy clubs, commerce promotions. Who in this today does not have the fantasy?

This is saga, it is romance, it is wonder. The first book is whole, some samples of it attachment. The second I create. I have total now twelve book titles, and all notions ready for the writing.

You may consider I will need use a text editor. My English is not very ideal. There is work to do. But brilliant stories will always shine.

All About Me

No. 1 New York Times *bestselling author George R. R. Martin has received every major literary prize for science-fiction or fantasy writing, including the Hugo, Nebula, World Fantasy, Bram Stoker, Daedelus and Locus awards.* Time *magazine has called him the American Tolkien. Christened George Raymond Martin, he added the extra initial when he was confirmed, aged thirteen, saying that he had arrived one R short. Martin shaped himself just the way he wanted.*

Indeed, just like snowflakes, no two potential authors are alike. Slushpiles reverberate with their proposals, presence and personalities. Asked to back up a proposal with relevant personal experience and qualifications, to say a bit about themselves, in a short biography, this is what they say.

- Do Not Consider Me as a Flawed Individual However I Actually Was Sentenced for Exhibiting Myself In a Public Place.

- With my life rushing bye, I have just reached double figures.

- I am the author of both reference books and articles ranging, respectively, from Business Spanish to the dramaturge Anton Chekov.

- My name initially is Joanna – I have written a book.

- I was once commissioned to produce a short animated film about a manatee that could talk.

- I am a multiple World Record holder with the *Limca Book of Records* but have been criminally ignored by the *Guinness World Records*.

- I am a pure artist and prepared to suffer for my craft, but I also need to pay the rent. I shed 7 kg producing this book and moved house twice. I can't afford to write another one until I earn something back.

- I have no previous experience in writing, so this is obviously my first bash. As it is written basically from my own experiences, it will be uniquely a one-off.

- I have read from almost before I was born.

- For me the pursuit of writing is intended both as a hobby and a way of raising funds for my predilection for fast cars and martinis.

- I am thirteen years old and have been writing from when I was young.

- After many years' studying astrophysics and earning my keep within giant international technology corporations, I am entirely convinced that I can become a commercially successful writer.

- I feel like I am a creative person who is awash with good ideas . . .

- I was brought up to put my faith in the power and strength of the Protestant ethic. I acquired an all-round love of competitive sports from my father, an accomplished equestrian, even though I was plagued by a series of phobias, including a fear of horses. I have nonetheless gone on to enjoy an action-packed life with taekwondo, jiu jitsu and shotokan karate, ice hockey and wrestling, which I performed to the very highest competitive levels.

- I grew up spending most of my time online. More recently I started to pay attention to the outside world a bit more regularly and this led to me being inspired to write.

- I guess that you get more unasked-for submissions than you could shake a book at.

- *As a devastating air crash throws its passengers into death's void, a roaring inferno guts the Paolozzi's pizzeria, and cold-blooded carnage culls the country's cattle. . . .* I am very keen to establish my position in the market as a vibrant, thrusting, young writer, who can grab the reader by the throat and not let go until the last page is turned . . .

- As a self-made fictional writer . . .

- I am retired and living in France, but still firing on all cylinders. I am more aware than ever that there is still much to do, including getting my guide to overseas caravan holidays published.

- I have had many joys and many sadnesses in my life. I have been a family man and a nobody. At this time I have been instructed by the Lord to make these things known to you.

- I have thought long and hard, but I can't think of anyone more able than me to write this book.

- If it would expedite matters, I'll supply a CV – although it's not going to be utterly truthful for reasons that will be obvious from my submission synopsis, which I admit isn't very informative.

- Previous experience *[for a crime novel]* includes a self-published guide to watercolours and a cookery book. *[And, more pertinently]* I have also worked in the police force and know just about all there is to know about fingerprinting and suspect profiling.

- I am not entirely sure that you will want to publish an aged author with a solitary script to sell?

- I used to sell encyclopaedias, floating floors, cockroach pesticides, linseed, opium and solar panels, with a stint in an auction house and a few years on booze cruises. I have since worked in insurance for more than 40 years, although I have been a scribbler from my very first school.

- As someone who considers myself something of a connoisseur in terms of literary taste, I am always amazed by the paucity of contemporary authors who are able both to write acceptable grammar and to tell a good story.

- My name is Marigold Shelley . . . I am highly spiritual; I have been told that I was Mary Shelley in a previous lifetime.

- I was once almost published in a literary magazine . . .

- Does any of this personal stuff wash? Look at some of the great writers. Kafka was bullied all his life by his father. Kenneth Grahame worked in a bank. Chekhov, like Margaret Thatcher, was a grocer's child; his grandfather was a serf. But if you must know, I have had a long career in accountancy, specialising in tax affairs.

- You will be able to tell that I am neither a literary expert nor a publishing insider. However, I have a great deal of experience as a reader and I am certain that I have paid good money for books that turned out to be considerably worse than the one that I would like you to consider for your list.

- I believe that people have been waiting for one single individual who can change the world. And I am that person . . .

- For my years *[85]*, I am in good health but conscious of the fact that I am currently loitering in the departure lounge of life. And that gives me a strong desire to leave something behind me.

- I get most of my ideas from the TV and this one is in no way an exception.

- I have written a commercial fiction, a story that echoes my life and career. I started it many years ago, but neglected to finish it because I succumbed to various addictions and subsequently had to mark time through a couple of prison sentences . . .

- I am at ease in interview, with public speaking and blatant yet charming self-promotion.

- I have a natural ability for writing page-turning thrillers that hook the readers from the off and then cartwheel through the plot at supersonic speed and end with a huge bang not a whimper.

- I am newly graduated from a college in the Black Country with a First in War Studies & Philosophy.

- I have recently moved to the Scottish Borders, where I spend my time teaching my dogs agility, gardening, writing, cooking and walking.

- I must admit to being a great-aunt . . . Regretfully, I don't fit the box labelled highly promotable young talent.

- I imagine that I am probably one of far too many writing material on alien abductions just now.

- I am what any publisher needs, a good, solid writer, an entirely safe pair of hands – think of me as being a cheese sandwich, a good hearty snack rather than a fine gourmet meal.

- Dispatched from the heart & mind of Gavin Banks. The brain of Donald Duck. The libido of Frank Harris.

- I have a lifelong interest in the subject of railways and transportation, being a traveller with wide interests.

- I am keen to learn and want this to be the first of several books as I already have other ideas for other future books. All I will tell you at this stage is that the name of the next book begins with the Letter S.

- I have a rickety past. I have lived life; indeed, I still do.

- My name is John Smith, and I am a 43-year-old writer. I come from Nuneaton. Well, somebody has to . . .

- I am co-writing with an author who is Enchantingly creative. We need one ADVENTUROUS publisher to MAKE THINGS HAPPEN. For sure she will be one BIG Plus . . . She has true Star Qualities, I write with GREAT HEART.

- My heroes in the literary world are Robert Ludlum and Patrick O'Brian, but I wouldn't want you to assume I am claiming that I could ever write as well as them.

- I am who I am.

Publishing Against
the Odds

Some authors overcome extraordinary and extreme challenges to get published: Henri Charrière and Jack London among them. Few equal René Belbenoit.

While French convict Henri Charrière's bestseller *Papillon* is among the finest prison memoirs, less celebrated but just as stirring is Belbenoit's *Dry Guillotine: Fifteen Years Among the Living Dead*. His book records the decade-and-a-half that he spent in the tropical penal colony of Saint-Laurent du Maroni, infamous for its brutal conditions and scores of political prisoners, as well as murderers and felons (among them Charrière). So horrific was Belbenoit's prison experience there that his military service as a teenager in the First World War paled by comparison.

Discharged after the war, Belbenoit worked in various low-paid jobs but at some stage was arrested for stealing, first a wallet then a necklace. Sentenced to eight years' hard labour, he arrived in Saint-Laurent du Maroni on the western edge of French Guyana in 1923. Of the 70,000 men and women dispatched there between 1852 and 1938, a third succumbed to typhoid, malaria, yellow fever, snake bites or leprosy; disowned, for the shame of it, many never saw their families again. Unsurprisingly, Belbenoit tried to escape several times, and after the third attempt he was dispatched to Devil's Island, some eight miles out to sea, enduring six months' solitary confinement in a place that housed those considered the colony's most dangerous prisoners.

Belbenoit began writing about prison life in 1926, although his guards often destroyed what he wrote. Undaunted, he would rewrite what was lost, able eventually to entrust his memoir to the safe-keeping of a local nunnery; always retrieving it whenever he made a bid for freedom. His fifth escape, in 1935, along with five others, involved almost three weeks at sea in a 19-foot boat; walking vast stretches of the inhospitable mountain and deep jungle terrain of coastal Central America. Eventually he managed to stow away on a ship bound for Los Angeles, arriving in North America in 1937.

On publication in 1938, Belbenoit's memoir became so successful that it was soon translated and published in several foreign-language editions. A welcome side-effect of its great success was the contribution it made to France's decision to end its transportation policy. And Belbenoit's dedication to becoming a published author is salutary. While on the run he had hacked his way through dense jungle on foot, travelled on horseback and by pirogue, traversed mountain ranges and braved fierce seas, all the while with his 30lb-manuscript, wrapped in protective oilskin, strapped to his side.

What's Your USP?

Not everyone's USP is as evident as René Belbenoit's. But everyone needs a unique selling point, that singular something that makes their book stand out, irresistible and one in a million; that gives it that artistic and commercial leg-up and essential je ne sais quoi.

How then to persuade a publisher that your book is worthy of support; that it will engage a reader with a captivating and involving story that keeps them hungry for more? Here are a few examples, plucked from the slushpile, of what some have decided makes their perfect pitch.

I have developed a style of writing which is unprecedented in human history. No mortal has ever written in this way before. God's blessings are indeed plentiful.

I have produced what I know is undoubtedly an incredibly good novel and will certainly turn into a bestseller and a future classic – with film and TV potential. The book has a happy ending.

This is a book just about me, an ordinary chap and how I get by in life, obstinately dodging the mud pies that the world throws at me.

I have been told that I am an alchemist. My writing can conjure golden success from base ingredients . . .

This is the best book ever, the greatest story ever told, and if you don't say you want to publish it you'll eternally rue the day you turned it down.

I would appreciate your consideration of the enclosed proposal for a humerous book, which I believe will achieve cult status. It might not sound funny but it is.

Keep a weather eye out for frequent random nudity, dark pointless humour and much unabridged swearing.

The book is special in a smart way. You can't stop turning the pages. Or put it down until the very end where the whole plot is revealed and the logical reasoning of what happened and why.

A book to be dipped into, carried around in your pocket, read on a train, dropped in the bath.

It is the first in a series of seven novels that will fill the yawning void at the heart of the literary and political establishment, and offer unique perspectives on hitherto 'untouchable' industries and institutions. If you believe in received concepts such as money, class, intelligence and 'the underclass', prepare to have your cosy assumptions blown to smithereens.

On the bookshelf it would be positioned somewhere in between *Eat, Pray Love* and *Fifty Shades of Grey* . . .

Imagine *Eat, Pray, Love*, but for men and the UK market – more plausible and less whacky, out of control, off the wall, emotional. Similar to *Zen & the Art of Motorcycle Maintenance* and *The Shack* with resonances of Eckhart Tolle.

I hope my travel memoir appeals to you. Think of it as Elizabeth Gilbert's *Eat, Pray, Love* meets Martha Gellhorn's *Travels With Myself and Another* . . .

. . . like a funnier version of *Eat, Pray Love* but with a strong undercurrent of Scandinavian irony (my mother was from Finland) . . .

If I am forced to compare it to some other book already in the market, I would say it could be similar to *Eat, Pray, Love* . . . but it's much, much better ☺

If all my readers, simultaneously around the globe, each began to think differently on reading my book, then that would be a huge shift towards making the Earth a better place to live. And if the light goes on for only one solitary reader, it could still be like the proverbial butterfly who flaps their wings on one continent and it leads to a hurricane of change ten thousand miles away.

The book is designed to appeal to the same readers as Jack Frost. I added very carefully some humour . . . Now please turn to first chapter if you dare. And I do hope that you enjoy reading this book as much as I enjoyed the making of it.

No one in mainstream publishing has been emboldened to tell the UK the truth about what the Bilderberg Group is doing to their nation – until now.

It is impossible to put down & gripping beyond words.

There is a gaping gap in the market for someone with my loopy sense of humour.

I have a massive hunch that this book will be a global hit. *[When no response is immediately forthcoming, the next day brings a message with a change of tone:]* It appears that no-one at your crappy company is able to read English. Or is my writing just too difficult and significant for your tiny minds to grasp?

After a great deal of research in bookshops and libraries and extensively surfing the internet, my conclusion is that I have written a book that will perform best in the downstairs loo.

My book might not appeal to you but if so all is not lost, because I am enclosing my author photograph *[attached with a paperclip]*; as you will see I am strikingly good looking.

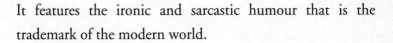

It features the ironic and sarcastic humour that is the trademark of the modern world.

People don't have much time for reading these days, so I have split my book into bite-size chunks, so that it will be easy for anyone, even with limited time, to consume a section a day without developing indigestion.

You ask about titles that are similar. I have racked my brains for days but have come to the inescapable conclusion that there are none.

While I could list numerous books about George Eliot, there are virtually none about the period she spent living in Coventry; therefore, I believe this book would have great commercial potential.

This book is a classic of the singular contemporary romance genre. The novel's heroine is of a special kind than is usual. There is sex and murder. Features thrilling adventures. Much sophisticated, top-notch romance. Set in land-locked Burundi. Has poetry and prose, myths and legends. Has extraordinary talents. *Has everything [ed.]*

I'm twenty-two. Think of my story as being about all the terrible mistakes I have made in my life and how to avoid them. Would you be interested in my kind of book?

The shelves of bookshops are groaning under the weight of self-help titles. But the irony is that none of those books really helps anyone. None of them shouts at you 'Start reading this book right now or nothing will ever change in your life and you are doomed to continue running around that hamster wheel until you die!'.

I accept that I will need some help in marketing the book and that you may want to hire someone to rewrite it.

The Secret Diary of a Loafer is exactly what it says it is: the secret diary of a loafer.

If you commit to publishing the book, you will successfully associate yourself with my extraordinary achievements and my potential to become a leader among men.

It is entirely possible that my novel is unique . . .

The major factor of this book is my inimitable, unparalleled wit and touch of the blarney.

I have been strongly advised by family and friends to write this story, so my unparalleled, exceptional life will be set down for eternity and never be forgotten.

Would you be interested in publishing my travel guide to North Korea?

I have made the hero vertically challenged so that he relies on his brainpower and does not operate from any physical prowess or advantage.

This is an escorted tour of my life, a single existence that bridges the preceding centuries.

A few months of life with misery me, augmented by a diversity of engaging stories, such as Where I Went To School, a challenging look at whether private or state schools are best, and How I Spent My Summer Holiday This Year, a scintillating story of the pros and cons of holidaying abroad or at home.

From the off, I wanted to write a book that is not only exquisitely written but also ingeniously plotted. I also wanted to create something that I could imagine stacked up in piles in an airport bookstore – to sum up as briefly as possible, 'a rattling good read'.

A story of Manichean good versus evil, with truly moral questions being examined through the lens of a good old-fashioned serial-killer story.

It's a playful, entertaining mix of Famous Five, *The Beach* and Cormac McCarthy's *The Road* with a dash of Diggers and dreamers.

My book will serve as a warning to some, a manifesto to others and a battlecry to the rest.

There have been few, if any, exclusive biographical studies of this quite remarkable anthropologist.

Here is the proposal for my how-to guide that will give people all the tools and inspiration they need to fulfil their travel dreams, FLY DOWN THE AMAZON. . . This is no ordinary memoir.

If there is a single moral to the story it is 'keep examining your faith', to which might be added 'and when you have done that examine it again.'

What makes this memoir special is my outstanding eye for detail and a photographic memory, which all add up to make me a prose writer of unusual distinction.

I have had it produced and printed, designed the cover & sold numerous copies with excellent feedback *[but forgotten to include any reviews or sales figures]*.

Part 3

Jack Kerouac was an avid reader, who knew by the age of ten that he wanted to be a writer. As a teenager he wrote stories and kept a journal, but his breakthrough 'spontaneous prose', as his trademark style became known, came with his second novel, On the Road. *Although dismissed as 'typing' by his contemporary Truman Capote, Kerouac revised and edited the typescript of the novel that made his name over many years from the late 1940s, rewriting constantly. In one three-week period, in April 1951, he sat at a typewriter and rewrote the novel on rolls of teletype paper without paragraphing or double spacing. The scroll still exists. Taped together, it comes in at 120 feet – something that would make a splash in any slushpile.*

Dear Team Publishing

I have written and ready to publish nine unpublished Nathaniel Coulter novels, the first of which is:

Nathaniel Coulter & the Silver Sword.

For sure, I am in no way trying to emulate any previous books about magic and suchlike. Each author has his own unique style and there can be no comparison between these and other titles.

So who is this Nathaniel, you must be wondering? He is a modern hero who has discovered how to tame his magical powers to take on all kinds of drunkenness, toadyism, lechery, sloth, murder, cowardice. He has a wand from which he can emit a corrosive liquid that 'devours' the human face, and a wallet which, if pressed in a special manner would explode spewing a sternutartious, diuretic gas. Because of his many confrontations with the forces of evil, he hears of a special school that his parents don't know of, where he learns many magical lessons.

I can reveal that the other titles in this unique series will be:

Nathaniel Coulter & the Empty Quarter
Nathaniel Coulter in Somerset
Nathaniel Coulter & the Big Dune
Nathaniel Coulter & the Egyptian Hieroglyph

Nathaniel Coulter & the Chocolate Croissant
Nathaniel Coulter & the Giant Stalactite
Nathaniel Coulter at the Durdle Door
Nathaniel Coulter & the Frozen Antelope

Most Estimable Publisher

At this initial early phase of our hopefully extensive dialogue I should like to humbly profess how unequalled a deep personal privilege it is for me to be in correspondence with you.

Dear Sir

I would have e-mailed you, but I am not allowed access to such facilities as I have just been sentenced. I shall be in touch again as soon as I can, but I can't count on it . . .

Can I interest you in my proposal, *The Tabernacles, Chapels & Churches of South Wales*?

My research for this book involved asking everyone I met over the course of a year the key question: which is your favourite chapel/tabernacle/church in South Wales? It is a question that, admittedly, was sometimes met with a degree of puzzlement and a blank look. But, nothing ventured, nothing gained. These Welsh landmarks are slowly being lost, as many as one a week, and there is a concern that hundreds more may have to close their doors for ever due to lack of interest and falling numbers of worshippers.

We need a record of our historic places before it is too late, and they are all converted into holiday homes or allowed to crumble. And the book that I propose to write would provide it.

From an exhaustive search of the books at your table, I have determined that this one's for you:

Four Irrefutably Tangential Lives and Overlapping Worlds: Theodore Roosevelt, Edgar Rice Burroughs, Maharishi Mahesh Yogi and Alfred Hitchcock.

Hallo one and all

My name is Frank. I have been emboldened to write to you because I believe there is a big gap in the thriller genre now that Ian Fleming has passed away.

I could never match the genius of Mr James Bond, but inspired by his exploits, here are twenty-seven story's, stings in the tale mostly, each about 9,000 words long.

I am not good at dialogue or character, but all my readers tell me that I know how to tell a ripping yarn and once they start to read my work they can't stop. I appreciate your time is precious. But, before I go, here is a little taster;

As the burning tyre rolled slowly down the road towards the mini-bus. As the children looked in horror, fearing their young lives were only seconds from being extinguished, a tall, angular figure strolled out from the café and kicked the tyre safely into touch, before casually settling back down to finish his latte.

Thank you for your trouble.

It would be an unrivalled delight for me, if you were to be so kind as to proffer any comment which might help me on my personal the journey towards the light, with regard to my Book of Short Stories (1752 pages), entitled, The High and the Mighty: Love, Fraternity, Value and Nobility and the Various Relations Between Earthly Powers.

Dear Editor

Initially may I say how sorry I am for not getting this to you more quickly following our email exchange last month about my book, however, a spate of deaths in the family, as well as a flood in the family home, led to an unfortunate delay.

I am a fifty-year-old pastor and healing spirit guide … I am presently seeking a publisher for my debut novel, *My Secret Life*. It follows the strange imaginary adventures of a man who is stuck in a profession he hates, and finds his only release is to escape into reveries of invincibility and potency. It is not autobiographical.

Dear Madam

I wonder if I can excite your interest in my humorous parody of life in the academic world, entitled 'You Don't Have to Be a Bastard To Work Here But It Helps'?

Please find enclosed my first attempt at penning a bestseller.

You will find I have boiled it down to as few words as possible. I find it tiresome when writers pad their stories out with endless dialogue and too many narrative dead ends. Anything that doesn't move the story forward at a rapid pace should be consigned to the recycle bin as soon as it has been typed, rather than trying readers' patience with this verbal diarrhoea …

Hallo to the publishing team

I just want to let you know that my proposal for a book will be winging its way towards you shortly, so I hope you will be watching your pigeonhole in expectation.

Dear Publisher

Management for Megalomaniacs: Manage like Hitler, Motivate like Mao

Do you expect attention and admiration? Appear tough minded and unemotional? Believe yourself smarter and better than others? Expect to be acknowledged as superior and special? If so, you are probably a megalomaniac.

Megalomania has got a bad name. But without it, where would we be? A desire to reach the top and destroy the competition en route is evolutionarily useful. Don't most of our political and business leaders have megalomaniacal tendencies? Doesn't their supreme and aggressive self-confidence enable them to persuade the rest of us to follow them, often blindly? Why be contented and happy when you could rule the world.

This book teaches you how to recognise your megalomania as healthy, beneficial and natural. Don't see your anger, rage, bloodlust, impulsivity and impatience to influence, motivate and manage others as a problem or disorder, but use it to achieve what you want: wealth, power and influence. Allow yourself to get in touch with your delusional fantasies. Embrace them and create the world you want.

With advice from history's dictators – from Alexander the Great, Napoleon and Mussolini to Hitler, Pol Pot and Mao. Learn their lessons and heed their warnings.

This is a business book that means business. Cover suggestions are included.

Lee Burdon

It's a fictional novel about a man who asks his friend to do him a favour then, in return, requests that he help him to murder his wife.

I know it might sound a bit like *Strangers on a Train* but they know each other, so it's not, because they're not strangers.

I am called Chris

Over the past year I have lost 30 kg and succeeded in reducing my body fat by 25 per cent. In case you don't believe me, I am enclosing two photographs. One is how I looked before I lost the weight, the other is how I look now. You will see that I now look much more fit and healthy as a result.

I am considering writing a book about how I achieved this, a sort of inspirational book about my battle to lose weight, including all the details of my keep-fit regime, from meal planning and diet to lifestyle.

I sincerely believe that readers all over the world will be inspired by my story and what has happened to me. That my journey will encourage millions to transform their lives. Do you feel we can take this new publishing idea forward?

I wanted to tell you that I have written fifteen books – with twenty-two in the pipeline. Over time I will be as celebrated as J. K. Rowling, so it's going to be in your best interests to sign me up right now.

Dear Reader

Would you allow a submission by e-mail? I live in Italy and don't have any faith in the postal system. I believe they've dug a large pit somewhere in Europe, where they bury letters and parcels for the UK.

Ever hopeful you will oblige.

Ha! Ha! Hoaxes

Forget all legitimate approaches to publishers via the reader and so forth. If all else fails and the end of one's tether is reached, why not consider alternative routes to achieving one's goal? Over the years, there has been some inventive trickery to outwit the slush- and publishing-selection process and those who oversee it.

Doris Lessing

Lessing was a bestselling author, whose novel *The Golden Notebook*, published in 1962, had by the early 1980s sold some 900,000 copies in hardback. But as her publishing career progressed, and her books sold ever more copies, she became ever more aware of a publishing process that made it harder for unknown writers: with its tendency to get name fixated and a system that can be mechanical; the fact that an established author receives more automatic respect than anyone just starting out.

With this in mind, in 1982, in what has become a celebrated experiment to illustrate some of the hurdles facing aspiring authors, Lessing dispatched a couple of her unpublished novels to publishers under the pseudonym Jane Somers. The first book, *The Diary of a Good Neighbour*, went to three London publishers, one of whom was her regular publisher; of the two that rejected it, including her regular publisher, one deemed it 'commercially unviable'. Bought by the third, on publication the book sold adequately and received a few reviews – some describing it as a pale imitation of Doris Lessing. But its lukewarm reception seemed to support Lessing's wariness of the publishing process, in the sense that nothing succeeds like success; a book brought out under her name, in the wake of her success, was more likely to do well, whatever its merits.

William Boyd

In the late 1990s, William Boyd invented post-war American painter and enfant terrible Nat Tate, a reclusive genius, who had destroyed most of his own work and then, in 1960, aged thirty-two, killed himself. Boyd made Tate flesh in a book, in the detail of its footnotes and its German publication as an art monograph. He went to great lengths to make his invention real, creating surviving artwork and trawling junk shops for old photographs, which he captioned as Tate's family and friends. His own A-list friends, including David Bowie, Picasso's biographer John Richardson and novelist Gore Vidal, assisted by claiming, variously, to have known Tate and have collected his work, thereby providing high-end accreditation.

At the book's US launch party in Jeff Koons' Manhattan studio, some recalled a Tate retrospective; many lamented his premature death. The hoax was exposed prior to the London launch; fall-out followed. Tate, however, lived on, via three documentary films and as a minor character in his creator's fictional memoir, *Any Human Heart*. If, as is said, it was more the making real of something made-up than the hoax itself that fascinated Boyd, in that he succeeded.

Jane Austen

Would Jane Austen find a publisher or agent today? In the face of persistent failure to get his novel published, David Lassman, director of Bath's Jane Austen Festival, asked himself just that. In his search for an answer, as Alison Laydee, a play on Austen's pen name, A Lady, he submitted a synopsis and excerpts from *Susan* (*Northanger Abbey*) to some UK top publishers and agents. He changed the title and some other names too, and made other minor alterations. Among the rejections that followed, there was only one slushpile reader who identified Austen's work. Lassman repeated the experiment with *Persuasion*, retitled *The Watsons*, again receiving a slew of rejections, for reasons that included lack of commercial clout.

Pride and Prejudice was next (as *First Impressions*, an early title). Lassman changed some names, as before, although he kept the book's opening line. The universal rejection that ensued (except for a lone publisher who called his bluff) was disheartening and amusing in equal measure. The conclusion that Lassman reached as a result of his experiment was that literary agents and publishers were employing folk to assess their slushpiles who couldn't spot a good read when they saw one … (although, in their own defence, the publishing pace-setters claimed they'd been aware of the hoax but had had no desire to stoop to conquer or provide it with the oxygen of publicity).

Ern Malley

Ern Malley's poems featured in the Autumn 1944 issue of Australian art and literary magazine *Angry Penguins*. Shortly thereafter, they were exposed as a hoax, perpetrated by James McAuley and Harold Stewart, who had wanted to prove that what they saw as meaningless nonsense could be taken seriously by the avant-garde. McAuley and Stewart are said to have written the poems by opening books haphazardly and choosing a random word or phrase. Job done, they sent the poems to *Angry Penguins* editor, Max Harris, claiming to be the sister of the recently deceased Ern Malley. With the support of his colleagues, Harris published sixteen Malley poems in the magazine, pushing the boat out with a commemorative cover.

A Sydney newspaper exposed the prank, the first casualty of which was Harris, his reputation dented. Things went from bad to worse when some of the poems were deemed an infringement of the South Australian Police Act; Harris was successfully prosecuted for publishing 'indecent matter'. The hoax hit the international headlines and did little to help the cause of literary modernism and experimentation in Australian literature. But, ironically, the poems have survived, still an inspiration to artists and writers – and imitators.

Chuck Ross

Ross was an unpublished writer disillusioned with a publishing industry he saw as incapable of recognizing new talent – including his own. To establish this, he typed up a sample of National Book Award winner Jerzy Kosinski's *Steps* and sent it out to assorted publishers and agents – and got nowhere (an ironic twist in the tale is the later accusation of literary fraud levelled at Kosinski himself).

Spurred on perhaps by his previous hoaxing success, Ross then sent the screenplay for *Casablanca* to a selection of film agents – with an equally negative outcome.

I Before E Except
After C . . .

If the traditional route to publication is followed, accurate spelling, although not the sine qua non, is an aspect of a book submission that shows the writer cares enough to read it through – at least once. It gives a proposal a professional gloss. Badly spelled submissions distract from the main event and can encourage any reader to give up. If you can't be bothered to use Spell Check at least or give your proposal a quick proofread, will you stay the course?

But never fear, help is at hand with the German Lernstift or 'learning pen', which has a built-in sensor, software that recognizes writing movements and tracks the shape of the letters to recognize words. It then vibrates when a mistake is made. Lernstift also has integrated Wi-Fi; it can be connected to a smartphone or PC to upload written texts online, share them on social networks or take part in writing training.

In the meantime, a few mistakes do seem to creep into book proposals . . .

- There is defiantly a market for this genre . . .

- She opened the front door, and was suddenly blown a way.

- I am a debutting writer . . .

- You can find me dtales at the bottom of the page.

- He was an elderly gentleman, but so well-turned out and fragrant that he made the future seem palettable to those who encountered him.

- But of cause I should be trying to persuade you of my vertues as a writer!

- Please find attached the first chapter of one of my story's for your perusal.

- I have started a new project: writting seekwells to classics.

- As she turned the corner and looked up at the pealing, decreipt mansion her heart sank.

- Only now did he appreciate the enormity of the path a head.

- I will look foreword to your thoughts.

- The houses of the district are a good indication of there owners wealthy lifestyles.

- I will hope to here from you soon.

- As the music started, Liz's heart was all aflutter, as she watched the gentlemen in hansom attire.

- Harking back to it's glory day's ...

- Henry gazed at the crown, dizzy with the thought he'd finally be able too where it.

- She sat in oar and realised she was becoming bewhiched.

- The servants lived and (for the most part) worked below stares.

- This old depilatoried once grand now sorry for it's self hotel ...

- In Turkish cultures it is customary to celebrate a wedding with the entire extended family, but such customaries do have there drawbacks.

- The lake was quit a big size.

- The situation kept getting more ubsurbed.

- We need to be realisic.

- But your going to marry the man of your dreams.

- As they touched fingers, there blood mingled.

- This is a nice story, and I would defiantly read more by this writer. It is a nice style, I like the style.

- As I attempt to embark on a litirary career ...

Who Will Buy My Book?

Once upon a time, in Europe, particularly before the invention of the printing press and the establishment of paper-mills in the fifteenth century, books were beyond the reach of nearly everyone, the preserve of cathedrals, monasteries and the like. For a start, most people couldn't read or write. Furthermore, books were expensive to produce, taking a great deal of skilled work and animal skins (the sourcing, never mind the preparation, of parchment was a slow and complicated process). A book could take years to produce and end up costing as much as a farm.

Today, in Hereford Cathedral, the seventeenth-century Chained Library survives intact with all its chains, rods and locks. The most widespread and effective security system in European libraries from the Middle Ages to the eighteenth century, the practice of chaining books was done in such a way as to enable precious books to be read in situ *and not stolen.*

Today, illiteracy is not the norm, and books are throwaway, cheap as chips, with the book market ever more crowded. At the time when Canterbury Cathedral's library was a collection of just a few hundred books, it was considered a major library. Things are quite different now – and not just in Canterbury. Nielsen, the world's leading global-information and measurement company, compiles market research on virtually everything, including the publishing industry. By 2013, its database had more than 22.5 million title records, which equates to a lot of books. So how best to pinpoint the market for your own book and identify who is likely to part with some of their hard-earned cash in order to read it?

Richard and Judy would like this book. So would Cliff Richard. And HRH The Queen would definitely love it.

My audience would mostly consist of middle-aged, middle-brow, middle-class, middle-of-the-road readers.

This is for anyone who has ever been struck by the clarion call of realization that change is needed.

If you have ever wanted to just stand up and walk out on your job, this book's for you.

My cookery book is designed for anyone interested in food or eating.

For the reader whose mathematics and physics is at undergraduate level with a basic knowledge of number theory and combinatorics – essentially, the non-expert reader.

With gallons of fiction on tap for mid-life, Pinot Grigiot-drinking, Zumba-thumping, Bikram-yoga-bending book lovers, when you reach the bottom of the glass, the reality of what's on the shelves helps not one jot with the mundane, repetitive-strain injury of our existence. What you have here changes that.

Most people can see that our current economic system has failed – this book is for those readers who want to know exactly why the economy is in such bad shape and what we can do to fix it. It would also make a great film.

For anyone who has ever yearned for a good read.

The target market is those old enough to remember life before computers changed the way we communicate, plus anyone younger who is interested in how they changed our world.

This topic has developed over the last ten years and is now crucial reading for the general public at large, indeed to virtually, almost, everyone on two legs.

For the young-at-heart hedonist in all of us.

My target market would be the slightly older reader, which is why my book is rather short.

My wife/husband/mother/father/friends/family/lover/dog thinks this is a great read and should be published *[just for the record, no glowing endorsement from any of these will guarantee a book deal]*.

My book has great global potential, given that going after one's dreams has worldwide appeal.

I am grateful for the chance to share with you my first book . . . I believe the collective unconscious is currently ready to receive it warmly.

Ostensibly I am aiming at a highly intelligent readership who can process a deeply complex plot.

I feel that my book offers a balance of many things: primarily a first-rate mystery, it also features romance, shape-shifting, geographical relocation, and a great sense of fun.

This is for anyone who is interested in giving his/her life a sense of meaning.

Aimed at same punters as the Frost novels and M. C. Beaton ... Straightforward, easy reading for the not-so-young.

Isn't there room in the marketplace for folk who like to read widely, like I do? I enjoy everything from Dostoevsky, Aleister Crowley and Dickens, to Mills and Boon, P. D. James and Garrison Keillor. I'd like all that in one book, and, without blowing my own trumpet, here it is.

This is an erotic novel for any urbane, discerning, adult reader. It is clever, confrontational and well written. Perfect for those who are stuck in a vanilla existence, looking to spice things up in their imagination.

A book of humour and enlightenment, perfect for plane, boat, bus and train journeys.

Note on potential readership for my book: frankly, unlimited. Ideal for anyone looking for a mega page turner to lose themselves in.

This would appeal to the crossover between two demographics: that group of readers who are interested in cryptography and lovers of baroque architecture.

Advised by publishers that when composing a cover letter like this one I must compare what I have written to books already published and available, I discovered nothing similar. Am I out on a limb here in believing that I have written a trailblazing one-off?

This is not for fans of literary yawns like Donald Barthleme, Angela Carter or David Mitchell. Nor for aficionados of toe-curlingly cosy crime or fluffy female fiction. But it is for anyone who likes a fast-paced story, well written, a great good read.

For the baby boomers hanging out there, still shaking their rheumatic tootsies about, so to speak.

Anyone who enjoyed Harry Potter . . .

The primary audience for the book would be cinema lovers. The secondary audience would be those who have a good understanding of the ins and outs of market research and statistical analysis.

For all fans of Bridget Jones . . .

The audience would be readers of *The Da Vinci Code* . . .

The book would appeal to a crossover between lovers of Harry Potter and Bridget Jones, with a plot as fiendish as *The Da Vinci Code* . . .

My work potentially has a very wide readership among both adults and children. However I would be happy to rewrite it entirely for either adults or children if you prefer.

My target audience is people like myself, silver surfers who enjoy a jolly good read but don't want to end up with scrambled brains in the process.

Ideal for your customers – if they read me, they'll save themselves the hassle of looking elsewhere, where they are bound to be disappointed.

I have given the book extensive 'road-testing' among the target audience of teens. Teenagers do not pull their punches. They tell it like they see it, and my test readers universally saw it as a very good thing indeed.

Primarily young urban men who would read it on the Underground (and would be happy to be seen reading it there.)

My latest novel has been welcomed by a wide variety of readers, male and female, young and old, so this is precisely who I am targeting.

Virtually every woman from John O'Groats to Land's End will be queuing night and day around the clock to be first in line to buy a signed copy of this book!

I feel that my novel has any number of potential plots left, and that it would fit into most fiction lists. Or, should I say it would be equally incongruous no matter which fiction list it appeared on.

I cannot envisage any remaining gap not yet covered by hundreds of police procedurals on the shelves, including those that have made the journey to the small screen. So if we are being entirely candid, mine is merely another of many.

The human race generally has a morbid curiosity even if they don't readily fess up to it – so this is a hot topic with a massive potential readership.

The audience I seek is no-one in particular, just any basically bright reader.

For people who appreciate a good, old-fashioned, fun story with bawdy moments that will make them giggle and snigger out loud.

In our world now we must tap into the young and what makes us young at heart . . . [*A list of children's books, past and present, follows, from* Swallows & Amazons, Doctor Dolittle, Two from a Tea-pot *and* The Secret Garden *to* Watership Down, Hunger Games *and* Harry Potter.] Some of us have just forgotten. My book is an aide-memoire.

Part 4

The Brontë sisters had their own challenges with writing and getting published. Charlotte, Emily and Anne wrote under various pseudonyms, feeling the need to cloak their identities, given a widespread prejudice against female authors. The pen names that they generally used – Currer, Ellis and Acton Bell – had the same initials as each of their actual first names and surname, and none easily identifiable as male or female. (Their adopted first names were said to be the surnames of successful contemporary female authors.)

But gender wasn't their only obstacle. Living in the rural remoteness of the Yorkshire moorland village of Howarth, all the Brontës, including their brother Branwell, coped with isolation by creating their own entertainment. Mostly they wrote, making the best of limited practical resources. Like her siblings, Emily wrote on whatever she could find. Indeed, one reason given for the delay in subsequently publishing an edited collection of her poems was how hard it had been to read the minute, compressed script, scrawled on an assortment of odd-shaped scraps of paper.

The dearth of writing materials was no deterrent to Charlotte either. Inspired by Blackwood's Magazine, *a popular publication of the time, to which her father subscribed, she created* The Young Men's Magazine, Number 2, *dated August 1830. Written when she was only fourteen, almost two centuries later, in 2011, the manuscript sold at auction for £690,850. A mini miracle of nineteen hand-written pages, each 35x61mm, it is smaller than a credit card. On to these minute folios Charlotte squeezed more than 4,000 words – news, short stories, advertisements – creating an imaginary world for her own entertainment, one only able to be read with a magnifying glass. Such a feat has yet to be seen in any slushpile.*

Hullo

I would like to know what's happerned to my propsal because I haven't here frome you for to long time – was it you that called me Wednsday? If so would you ring back.

Please find enclosed the manuscript for MY FORGOTTEN YEARS, my recollections of life as an addict. It's not just another junkie memoir or post-heroin chic, more of a tale of woe and misfortune. I can remember some of what happened, but what I don't know I have made up. I am able to supply a fake cv, if required.

In this book I take a close look at consciousness and its half-sibling, the subconscious. I look at the way that we exist both within and without the body, in the now, the then, and the forever. I expect you would be able to get someone like Stephen Hawking to write an introduction for it.

My fictional writing, *Still Waters*, grew from one of the 4000 short stories I have accumulated from when I first started writing last year. I have now written six more novels, and a seventh is underway. Content covers humanity's ups and downs, from the sixteenth century to the present day, from murder to fantasy, horror and love. I have a publisher who is pestering me for more literature, but they're not up to the job and I am looking elsewhere.

This is the story of my six-month gap-year, during which I backpacked around the world. I am 100 per cent confident that this will be a successful book. I just need you, a renowned publishing company, to promote it.

Dear Sir or Madam,
I represent an author who is interested in submitting to you.

This is a novel written by myself over many yers, remembering that my englsih was not good today as good when I started. I am a native speker of Cantonese. Howver many Englsih, and Englsih speaking readers can ateest that my noveos is Vvery FINE LITERARTY QUALTY.

Here are some qestions for YOU.

A. How soon can you (usuall) get my bok piblish?

B. If my bok has few speling mistakes but the brilliance of plot and storyttlling outway the obstacle woud you find the virtues of the bok to overcome this hurdel?

C. Do you see a bok as good based on literarty qualty or on how similar book you publisherd before?

I aks these qestions because there was last year the case where an unown Taiwanese writer had his novl piblished by british publisher who paid advance of 250,000 Sterling Pounds (Yes, that is one quarter million pounds!!) And he's englsih was not half as good as myne.

To Whom It Might Ever Concern,

Here is a suspense thriller that delivers whipcrack after whipcrack of astonishment and passion, with a guaranteed flow of twists and turns which send extra shivers down the spine.

I have near perfect recall of my childhood and adolescence and have highlighted the many lessons learned along the way, in what I believe to be a deeply rewarding read. When my friends ask me about my book, I say that I have presented the story of my life as a little book of wisdom gleaned from each infinitesimal step along the long and winding road that leads between legacy, loss and lassitude.

Dear Mr or Ms

I am a chemist of some renown and the author of more than 150 textbooks on organic chemistry, including stereochemistry (study of the 3-D structure of molecules), medicinal chemistry (pharmaceuticals), organometallic and polymer chemistry. I am writing a book for the lay reader on the chemistry behind life's big questions, subjects of general, critical interest for science and religion. A sound knowledge of chemistry, to A-Level, is vital for all readers.

Dear Editors

While supping a pint or two at the Dirty Duck, I felt emboldened to take the first step in finding a publisher for my literary novel . . . It is written as an extended suicide note.

At heart, it's a memoir modelled on me, on my own messed-up life. The subject matter goes back to when I was, I am afraid, something of a lothario and a conman – a Casanova crossed with the Scarlet Pimpernel. I have attempt to write this story down many times before, but it was completely unpublishable till now and I wouldn't have been so silly as to waste your time with it. It still has some problems, but I am finally certain that, with a bit more effort, it would have great commercial potential.

It is a fantasy novel in the tradition of L. Ron Hubbard and the Dalai Lama a bit like but of course different from Doctor Who – but definitely not scifi.

It's planned as a trilogy, but can be extended, according to how many books you'd require.

I relish partnering with you to promote this story as well as the complete series which I will be happy to provide whenever you want.

The enclosed isn't a biographical book about my father . . .

A disappointed phone call about a slushpile submission comes in late June: I sent my novel to you in May – caller gives title & details, and reader a promise to look. But a subsequent search for the unread proposal finds no trace of it. Two months later, the missing proposal arrives via the post, delayed by the official-looking yellow sticker marked Revenue Protection. To pay: £1.50, 50p for deficient postage and a handling fee of £1.00.

Do you believe that you have lived before? If so, you are one of millions of believers in reincarnation.

In this saga, a quartet of characters engage repeatedly with each other over centuries, but in different forms. The narrative is thus extremely fluid and can take in such extremes as the battle for dominance in a dung beetle's world, samurai warriors in the middle ages, and the handmaidens to a French princess in 17th-century Avignon.

I see it as an interlocking series of twenty-one titles, which effectively tells the entire history of the world to date through the eyes of the four main characters.

You would simply not believe the indignitites and horrors inflicted on me by your fellow publishers over recent months. The cat-and-mouse games they have played with me, the lost manuscripts, the LIES and sheer INHUMANITY of it all. WHY CAN PEOPLE JUST NOT ADMIT THAT THEY HAVE LOST MY MANUSCRIPT?!>?

But I am a trusting type, so I start from the assumption that you must be better examples of the human race.

So, let me tell you about the book . . .

I appreciate that my subject is one that has been written about many times before. Since the book isn't yet written, I shall be pleased to shape its content as you might wish (Working title: *Fundamental Insanity*).

Here are my memoirs of the Swinging Sixties. I am the ideal person to document the period, because I am one of the ones who can actually remember it . . .

Can I interest you in *CLUCK! The fowl cookbook*?

Not a recipe book for hens, but a hundred fun ways to enjoy funky chicken dinners.

One of our healthiest meats – always a favourite – chicken takes on other flavours well. It's versatile too: you can roast it whole, barbecue it, make it into a pie, cheer it up with herbs and spices, turn it into a curry, casserole it as a one pot or eat it as fillets, leg or breast, with pasta, noodles or potatoes. Make chicken soup.

Whatever you do, though, don't eat it raw; otherwise there's nothing you can't do with chicken – and this book shows you.

Don't cry fowl on this one!

Dear Publisher

I found your contact details on your website, where it advises that you are happy to accept unsolicited manuscripts. Please find enclosed the few thirty pages of my novel. Before you start, I should warn you that it is no great literary masterpiece or creative magnus opus.

Dear Reader ...

It's done and dusted. You are about to take the irrevocable first step and send your proposal to the publisher, that maker or breaker of dreams. You have printed your book submission, the required few chapters, and parcelled them up with a pithy synopsis. But before you send everything off, there is still that elusive cover letter to refine before you spark the sometimes long journey to getting published. Especially the key, thorny issue of how to address the person who will pull your submission from the envelope and read your opening salvo – who could hold your fate as a writer in their hands. Here are some ideas on forms of address. Of course, you could always consult Debrett's. *Or ignore the greetings' challenge and sail straight in.*

In the Lord's name: Hello

Respected organization . . .

Dear most honourable & beloved reader

Warmest winter wishes to you

Dear potential agent, friend and colleague

Peerless Publisher

Dear future colleagues

Hiya!

Dear Patron

Hi there

Respected and highly admired madams and sirs

Dear 'Reader'

Dear Sir or Ms

Hi Mega Team Publishing

Dear Sir/Sirs/Mssrs

Dear Madam/Ms

Hi Trust you are all keeping well

Dear Publisher: How are you doing?

Dear Editor

Good day to you from John O'Groats

Hello & greetings

To whomever this may concern: I'd like to start by saying a little something about myself . . .

Hello Dear Clients and Friends

Dear Sir/Madame

Welcome to the 'Publisher' in UK

Most Highly Esteemed Mesdames

☺ ☺ ☺ ☺ ☺

Gold Slush

Is the slushpile really a graveyard? The place where work by hopeful new writers is laid to rest? Or does something sometimes come of the unpublished books sent off into the big dark without a torch? What follows are some heartening slushpile successes, successful authors who have triumphed over publishers' initial rejection or disinterest.

Malorie Blackman

Before she was published and long before she became Waterstone's Children's Laureate, 2013–15, Malorie Blackman once met Alice Walker at a book signing. Clutching a copy of one of Walker's books, Blackman asked Walker to inscribe it with the words 'Don't give up'. Indeed, Blackman did not give up, despite the eighty-two rejection letters she received for various books until *Not So Stupid!*, a collection of short stories for teenagers, came out in 1990. Blackman has said that trying and failing is better than never having the guts to try; when life knocks you down, keep getting up. The title of Children's Laureate is awarded to a celebrated author (or illustrator) in recognition of their outstanding contribution to their field, in Blackman's case as the author of more than sixty books for young readers; in 2008, she received the OBE for her services to children's literature.

Elizabeth Bowen

In 1927, Constable acquired *The Hotel*, a first novel by the young Anglo-Irish writer Elizabeth Bowen (1899–1973), after a recommendation by its slushpile reader Rose Macaulay, herself a published writer. What ensued was a long and distinguished writing career; in 1948, Bowen was awarded the CBE and further honours followed. *The Hotel* is now a Penguin Twentieth-Century Modern Classic.

Bill Bryson

Found in the Heinemann slushpile by its publisher's reader Heather Godwin, Bill Bryson's *The Lost Continent* (1989) has become a classic of travel literature. Bryson's subsequent raft of bestsellers includes *A Walk in the Woods*, *Notes from a Small Island*, *In a Sunburned Country*, *Bryson's Dictionary of Troublesome Words*, *A Short History of Nearly Everything* (which earned him the 2004 Aventis Prize) and *The Life and Times of the Thunderbolt Kid*. In 2006, he was awarded an honorary OBE for services to literature. By 2013, he was declared the UK's biggest-selling non-fiction author since official records began.

Mary Cahill

Three rejections into the submissions process, Cahill's literary agent advised her to jettison her new novel and start afresh. But Cahill ignored this advice, opting to agent herself. Of the seven publishers to whom she sent her murder mystery, *Carpool: A Novel of Suburban Frustration*, six sent it back. Failure beckoned until its potential was finally recognized, and the published book went on to become a bestseller and a Literary Guild selection.

Roddy Doyle

Spotted by the same reader, Heather Godwin, who discovered Bill Bryson, Roddy Doyle is now seen as one of Ireland's greatest living writers and his first novel, *The Commitments*, is a world-wide bestseller. It was also the first of his books to be adapted, in 1991, for cinema, with a script co-written by Doyle; the stage adaptation opened in London's West End in 2013. Post *Commitments*, Doyle has written many other books, including several novels, a collection of stories, a memoir of his parents and numerous books for children. He received the Booker Prize, in 1993, for *Paddy Clarke Ha Ha Ha*.

Michèle Forbes

The typescript of *Ghost Moth*, Forbes' first novel, which she wrote over three years between acting jobs, was turned down by thirty-eight UK and Irish publishers before it was bought by an American publisher and became the subject of a bidding war in the UK.

Anne Frank

Frank's *Diary of a Young Girl* was generally on offer following publication in Holland. At Doubleday's Paris office, it was spotted by Judith Jones, then a junior employee or what was known at that time as a girl Friday. Despite her lowly position, Jones was convinced of the book's merits and determined to get it published. Once Doubleday's New York office was on side, the English-language edition came out in 1952 – seven years after Frank had died, aged fifteen, in Bergen-Belsen.

Judith Guest

When Guest first sent out *Ordinary People* in 1975, it was knocked back by a couple of publishers, one of whom, she recalls, felt its satiric bite did not compensate for its overall failure to keep the reader engaged. Guest then sent the novel to the Viking Press, who considered it for eight months before deciding to take it on. On publication, the book rewarded that decision, becoming a bestseller; the subsequent film adaptation, Robert Redford's directorial debut, was initially spurned by the Hollywood Studios, but went on to win an Oscar.

Jack Kerouac

After his first novel, *The Town and the City*, had come out in 1950, Kerouac struggled for years to get his second, *On the Road*, published. But following eventual publication by Viking in 1957, and a positive review in the *New York Times*, the book's publication was deemed historic. *On the Road* was an overnight bestseller and became the anthem of the beat generation; its author an icon for his times.

Paul Harding

Tinkers, Harding's debut novel, was widely rejected until New York publisher Bellevue Literary Press, picked it up, and the book subsequently won the Pulitzer Prize.

Stephenie Meyer

In 2003, Meyer, then unknown and unpublished, contacted the Writers House literary agency with her 130,000-word teenage-vampire saga. Unaware that agents expected YA (young-adult) fiction to average 40,000–60,000 words, an agency assistant invited Meyer to send it in. Of Meyer's numerous rejection letters for what was to become *Twilight*, one arrived after she had signed with the agency and gained a three-book publishing deal. It had taken her only six months to reach this point – from coming up with the idea and writing the book to getting an agent and publisher. A sequel, *Breaking Dawn*, sold 1.3 million copies on its first day of sale.

Roy Moxham

Found in the Constable slushpile and published in 2001, Roy Moxham's first book of nonfiction, *The Great Hedge of India*, tells the improbable story of one of the least-known aspects of Queen Victoria's India – a customs barrier 2300 miles long, most of it made of hedge, grown and policed by 1200 men to impose a salt tax. His search for what is probably the longest hedge in the world, of which most people, including eminent historians, knew nothing, still sells world wide. Moxham went on to write other books, including *Tea: Addiction Exploitation and Empire* (2003), later re-published as *A Brief History of Tea,* and *Outlaw: India's Bandit Queen and Me* (2010).

Denis O'Connor

Plucked out of the Constable slushpile, after an initial launch by Waterstone's bookshop in Newcastle, Denis O'Connor found mainstream success with *Paw Tracks in the Moonlight*, a story about a kitten called Toby Jug that he rescued from the snow. Three more books followed in what has become an internationally acclaimed series of enchanting books about the author, his animals, his life in rural Northumberland and the power of nature to heal.

James Patterson

Patterson has said that he found an element of encouragement and compassion in publishers' rejection letters, claiming they had helped him keep faith in his novel. More than a dozen publishers rejected what became *The Thomas Berryman Number* before his literary agent, whom Patterson found via a newspaper article, sold it to Little, Brown. When Patterson visited the publisher's Boston office, he noticed some of its other authors' books on display, including J. D. Salinger's *The Catcher in the Rye*, John Fowles' *The French Lieutenant's Woman* and Norman Mailer's *The Executioner's Song*. He could scarcely believe he was about to join them.

Anne Plichota & Cendrine Wolf

The first book, *The Last Hope*, in Plichota & Wolf's bestselling children's fantasy–adventure Oksa Pollock series from France was aptly named. For co-authors Plichota and Wolf, their last hope was to self-publish, following zero interest from French publishers in series featuring much juvenile wizardry and a feisty thirteen-year-old heroine. Preferring a traditional print approach, they learned how to produce and promote their own books. Over two years they sold 15,000 copies, partly by selling direct to schools and libraries. By year three, when Pollockmania was raging throughout France, they secured a world-rights deal; book rights were then sold in twenty-seven countries and the producer of the *Twilight* movies bought the film rights – in other words, they had a full house.

Marcel Proust

Swann's Way, Proust's first book in his seven-volume novel, *Remembrance of Things Past*, celebrated its centenary in November 2013. But what is now hailed as a classic was spurned by the reputable publishers of its time. André Gide, dismissing Proust as a 'snob' and a 'social butterfly', a mere recorder of dreary high-society events, turned it down for his publishing house (later recalling this as 'the gravest error' and 'one of the most burning regrets, remorses, of my life'). Proust's brother reported that a reader at Ollendorff publishers had told him: 'My dear friend, perhaps I am dense, but I just don't understand why a man should take thirty pages to describe how he turns over in bed before he goes to sleep. It made my head swim.' Proust finally dipped into his own pocket to get his magnum opus published (by Eugene Grasset). Today, he might have considered the ebook self-publishing option.

Nora Roberts

Roberts' *The Irish Thoroughbred*, a horse-breeding tale set in Maryland, was rescued from the slushpile after three years of rejection and, in 1981, became her first published romance. Now hailed as a doyenne of romantic fiction, Roberts has 180 *New York Times* bestsellers to her name, including 30 as J. D. Robb.

Laurence Sterne

The first two volumes of Sterne's *Tristram Shandy* attracted no publishing interest. Sterne's faith in himself was rewarded when, on having it privately printed and published, the novel hit the jackpot and became a huge success. However, the book remained controversial, with Dr Johnson rejecting it as odd; claiming it would not last. But Sterne, who described his desire to write, 'not to be fed but to be famous', proved him and his other critics wrong.

Kathryn Stockett

Stockett's first novel *The Help*, which took her five years to write, was turned down some sixty times. The seemingly relentless stream of rejection letters included the advice that there was no market for 'such tiring writing'. But Stockett's refusal to admit defeat, despite general encouragement to do so, was rewarded when *The Help* was published and soared up the bestseller charts; later adapted for the screen. On her website Stockett cites two key tools for all writers: tenacity and a mentor.

It's Goodbye from Me

How to sign off? What follows are some memorable adieus as well as a few regrets & sometimes furious author feedback from those in receipt of the dreaded yet sometimes anticipated publisher's rejection letter.

Thanks in advance for taking the time to look at this, even if it does end up with you playing the Roman emperor and turning your thumbs down, while I die a gladatorial death in the dust down below.

You needn't send anything back. However I have enclosed a SAE for your letter offering me a book deal.

Beware, the spiralling concepts and trains of thought in this book may leave you in a spin for weeks after reading it.

Best wishes from Neasden's answer to Alan Titchmarsh . . .

This tale of psychological horror has been haunting my dreams for years now. I felt the best way to exorcise the fear was to write it down and pass it on to you.

My friend Bernadette and I have been on a journey of spiritual recovery around Europe and South America, seeking out ancient standing stones and relics. If you would like to see a proposal for a mixed travelogue/revelation of divine mystery, please contact me at the PO Box address above.

As an eternal optimist, I will continue to hope that you will be the publisher who decides to give me a contract.

I can only start to imagine how exciting it would be if you were to do me the honour of agreeing to represent my work.

I will look forward to hearing whether you will take up my offer – otherwise not.

I am intensely proud of this book and hope that it provides you with at least some mild amusement.

May the blessings fall from the stars on all your strivings here, and also in other worlds, times and states of being.

If you don't like this one, I am working on several more books, so will be in touch soon.

This is my first attempt at a novel, but I have six other unpublished non-fiction titles, including an idea for a biography of a well-known serial killer and a glamorous supermodel.

I will be waiting attentively on your reply. Until then, I am at your disposal.

Hoping that we have a lovely autumn. And also hoping to hear back from you before Christmas.

I am delighted that you are able to take the time to look at my submission. I am keeping everything crossed in the hope of a favourable outcome.

I understand that time is precious to you so I am determined to waste as little of it as possible.

I am now off to face the slings and arrows of daily life, happy in the knowledge that you will at least do me the honour of glancing through my book.

I am trying hard to keep this brief . . . *[towards the end of a **very** long letter]*

If you require any other form of submission from me, please don't hesitate to give me your instructions.

I firmly believe that, given a halfway competent editor and PR department, this book could have great prospects.

I have a great regard for the history of your publishing firm, and would be very pleased to join the distinguished ranks of your authors.

The name used to write erotica and thrillers is my real one.
The one I have used to sign this letter isn't.

Thank you for your attention
Sincerely
James Lee Burrows AKA William Lee Burroughs III

I hope that you will be richly blessed in your career and in all
your other strivings in the years ahead.

I will be excited to hear your verdict on my efforts. *[No return
address supplied]*

I hope that you see the same virtues in my book that I do. Warmest regards.

I have had several offers to publish it as an ebook, but I see it as much too good to be limited to the digital realm and believe it deserves to at least have a single small print run from a real publisher like yourself.

I hope you enjoy it and pray that we can build a strong relationship together.

Thank you for your comments on the first three chapters of *Lazy Days & Highs*, although I am disappointed that you didn't want to see more. For your information, the sex really gets going later in the book. Would you like to see just a few more chapters?

While for some the party's over, tomorrow's still another day for others, and the show goes on. There's always another book to write and a new letter to send – hope springs eternal.

Thanks for your detailed critique of my book. While it was rather negative, it was very interesting to hear the reasons for your decision. I also understand that the current economic climate is less than ideal for taking on debut authors such as myself and that you have to consider your possible losses. Would it make any difference if I were to put up £1500 to cover your initial costs, thus making the book a win-win investment for you?

Thank you for your kind letter. I am furious with myself for having pitched the book in such a hurry rather than showing a bit more patience. I now realise that it is always best to write the introduction after the book is complete, and I have now rewritten the intro so that it perfectly captures and reflects the mood of the book, so I hope you won't mind me resubmitting my proposal?

Happy Holiday Season and many thanks for your thoughtfull comments on the material I submitted. Your analysis of the lack of commercial viability of the work was spot on in my opinion. In order to address this, I have decided to rename the book, reduce the word count to the bare minimum and self-publish it as an ebook in order to reach the target market of geeks, drop-outs and techno addicts.

The letter I sent with my book submission was really not adequate for the task, so please read this one instead.

Was it actually you who wrote to me, or was it an apparatchik churning out rejections and attaching your name to them? If you wrote it yourself, then I am appalled at the obnoxious, negative tone of your remarks.

I appreciate your notes on the chapters I sent. I see now that most of the first half of the book is actually redundant, while the real quality lies in the latter half, which you haven't seen. But I feel that now I have poisoned the well by sending a half-cocked attempt there is no point in resending the remaining material.

Perhaps I didn't explain the book clearly enough.

I am not sure what gives you the divine right to foist your uninformed opinions on the rest of us?

If you failed to appreciate this book it is your fault and nobody else's.

Mark my words, I will be complaining to the Society of Authors.

I wonder how all those editors who turned down J. K. Rowling are feeling now. It must be very uncomfortable to be known as the editor who rejected the next big thing.

Standards at your publishing house seem to me to be very poor indeed. I don't know why I bothered.

How could you do something like this?

Go straight to hell.

The A–Z of How
Not to Get Published

This easy-reference guide to the pitfalls of getting published comes with a cast-iron, copper-bottomed guarantee that publication will remain a pipedream.

address
Send in your book idea to a publisher, but be sure not to include any contact details – no postal or e-mail address, landline or mobile number; do not supply any means whatsoever of their getting in touch or reaching you. That's how you can be sure never to hear from any of those pesky publishers ever again.

adjectives
Use liberally; so liberally that the text can't move for them.

adverbs
See ADJECTIVES.

anniversaries
Wait until just before a major, newsworthy date of a landmark historical event, say a centenary, for example, of a major war,

or a celebrity-led anniversary, then contact the publisher with your exquisitely ill-timed proposal.

Given that publishers need a while to arrange things – to read and absorb your idea or book and take it to a commissioning meeting for agreement (or not) to publish; then, once it's written and delivered, to initiate any rewrites, then read it again once amended; assign an editor for the text, a picture researcher for possible illustrations (for which permission to use must be cleared); get the cover and text designed, proof read arranged, index compiled, the book sent off for printing, binding and warehousing; never mind any publicity plans, marketing ideas and distribution arrangements organized – it is likely you'll be told no. Beware, however, because publishers can do things quickly, when they need to, for instance with books about nuclear disasters, such as Chernobyl.

argue

To banish the inner calm that can help you to write. Equally, if you're too calm, too happy and never argue, this can induce lack of creativity. In the latter case, be sure to take up a hobby or two; apart from anything else, you'll be too busy ever to write a thing.

block

Develop writers' block or depression as a tried-and-tested method of stopping the creative flow.

bold

Make sure you have the reader's attention by typing in bold at every opportunity; whenever you feel you might be losing focus or not getting your point across. Or perhaps you are just an angry soul or possibly just short sighted. Bold up your entire book, just to make the point STRONGLY. Yes, use CAPS to up the ante, when you feel your words are flagging. See also CAPITAL LETTERS and ITALICS.

bore

If you bore yourself while you are writing, there is no chance you will entertain your readers; so, another useful trick to have up your sleeve in your mission not to be published. If you find yourself yawning, distracted and nodding off as you write, thinking about what you are going to have for lunch or whether you should put the washing on now so it will dry before you need it that evening, you're on the right track. Write entertainingly so time flies, and you could be in trouble.

bribes

For the publisher's reader, natch. Make them as big as possible – best, however, to avoid sending unsubtle stashes of cash. You could start with a chocolate bar tucked inside the submission envelope, although one that won't melt in transit (try a

CurlyWurly) or be pulverized (Flake). Or raise the stakes and offer the use of your chateau in Bavaria or Caribbean-based yacht; a Cornish cottage would do. But make sure the reader knows they will be expected to sing for their supper, as in help you to write your book.

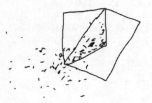

capital letters

TYPE OR, PREFERABLY, HAND-WRITE YOUR BOOK ENTIRELY IN CAPITAL LETTERS (IN PENCIL TOO, IF YOU LIKE). YOU WILL THEN BE DEEMED EITHER MAD, SOMEHOW INCARCERATED FOR YOUR OWN SAFETY OR THAT OF OTHERS, OR WELL KNOWN FOR YOUR PROPENSITY TO SHOUT – NONE OF WHICH IS A GOOD BET IN AN AUTHOR, FROM A PUBLISHER'S VIEWPOINT. OF COURSE, YOU MIGHT JUST SUFFER FROM MYOPIA, BUT DON'T ADMIT THAT EITHER.

clichés

Use hackneyed phrases and stereotypical trite expressions or cheesy characterisations, their effectiveness worn out through over-use, excessive familiarity and exposure.

collector's editions

Suggest a deluxe edition of the classic text, *Liber Chronicarum* by Hartmann Schedel printed in Nuremberg in 1493 (otherwise known as *The Nuremberg Chronicle*), the most extensively illustrated book of the fifteenth century. Propose a print run of 2500, on animal skins – goat or sheep – as a novelty purchase for the oligarch market, featuring Damien Hirst instead of Durer. As, among other challenges, this would require the pelts of 210,000 hapless creatures, it's hopeful there would be no takers.

copyright

Write a book about an extremely famous, internationally well-known person, perhaps another writer, who is still alive or whose estate still controls use of their work. Getting permission to quote copyright work/letters/diaries can be an uphill task, off-puttingly expensive and ultimately lead nowhere – as it did for biographer Ian Hamilton's book about J. D. Salinger, *A Writing Life*. That book never saw the light of day because, ultimately, Hamilton was subject to a legal ban regarding all Salinger's letters. Except that Hamilton was determined the book would be published; so he regrouped and rewrote the entire thing without infringing Salinger's copyright, and *In Search of J. D. Salinger* was widely praised on publication. So watch out for any determination that you might have if you decide to go this route. It might be your undoing and lead to a deal.

dialect

It might have worked in *Wuthering Heights* or *A Kestrel for a Knave*, but writing regional dialect or patois is fraught with danger. Unless extremely well done and sparsely used, it does not help express the voice; readers find it annoying. Perfect: if you don't want to be published, employ plenty of patois; even add, in brackets, an adjacent translation to slow down the narrative and bring the reader to a standstill. The fact is phonetically written dialect is so hard to read that it's likely no one will. So, spread it thick if you want your novel never to appear in print or never to be read. Do say: 'I'll 'appen that's it.' 'If ah don git di rent he go mek me peh.' 'I'll see youse.' 'Wah gwan?'

discipline

If you're employing an inner regimental sergeant major (as used by Will Self) who coerces you to get writing every day, then sack them immediately. Dispatch them to a war zone or someone keen to get their work published.

endings

Margaret Drabble's advice to writers is to keep at it; finish a novel rather than losing faith in it and starting a new one. But, with non-publication as a goal, never learn the lessons of getting to the end.

endorsements

Remember to include every rejection letter you have ever received from other publishers. It doesn't matter how long ago; in fact, the more decades back the better.

Or include praise from your mother/wife/children/nearests and dearests, claiming that they couldn't put it down (not with you standing over them with that look on your face, they couldn't) . . .

epic

To paraphrase Ambrose Bierce, author of *The Devil's Dictionary*, an epic is a book of which the covers are too far apart. The word count of the average book is somewhere between 60,000 and 100,000 words.

My book is 700,000 words and I have another six in the pipeline. Here's the first one ... I am planning a ten-volume series.

Overlong books can be off-putting, a point acknowledged by one slushpile author who included a tiny yellow post-it note on page 300 of a 600-page proposal that read: *'Well done for getting this far. You're half way now.'*

However, some long and successful books include:

- Marcel Proust's *Remembrance of Things Past* (in *Guinness World Records* as the longest novel, despite publication in several volumes)
- Robert Musil's *The Man without Qualities* (published as two volumes, though considered one book, is also very long, at about 1775 pages)
- Samuel Richardson's *Clarissa* (often described as the longest novel in the English language, but shorter than both the above)
- Leo Tolstoy's *War & Peace*, Victor Hugo's *Les Misérables*, Ayn Rand's cult classic *Atlas Shrugged*, Vikram Seth's *A Suitable Boy* and David Foster Wallace's *Infinite Jest*.

exclamation marks!
Use these all the time! Yes, that's right! Pepper your pages with these little lovelies, the sign of a writer drowning.

fake
Go the whole hog and create a fake, like the ultimate Jack the Ripper diary you might claim to have found in a wardrobe

or the basement of your new house or that fell from beneath the floorboards when you removed a ceiling. But learn from others' mistakes before you do this. Remember the 'Hitler Diaries', allegedly discovered in 1983 and announced by political magazine *Der Stern*. The *Sunday Times* bought the serial rights. But the diaries were found to be fake, when, under UV light, the paper used for them contained an optical brightener that had only been available some years after Hitler's death. See also HA! HA! HOAXES.

Facebook

Studiously ignore social media. Without it you won't be in the game. Retreat to your high moral ground and feel above it all. And alone, unpublished and unread.

foreign language

Submit your book idea in Chinese or Japanese. Make sure there is no English anywhere, not even in the covering letter. Pretty foolproof. Unlikely that the reader will be able to grasp a single word – especially given how famed the British are for not learning other languages. And they will not even be able to ask you if you'd like it back. So, zero contact.

Or, as a speaker of English as a second language, send in an idea that is so indecipherable that no one can make any sense of it. If English is your first language, let your hair down and pretend you can't speak a word of it, to make it more fun:

My prposed book is ministrted to the goodness of murthering and popery. In soving mystry and idnetifying the criminal the hero is, but of corse romance is of the esssnce. I hop you will considr submission mine.

gallivant

Go out; don't sit at your computer day in, day out, typing. Enjoy your life; go on a gap year; take a holiday. Say to yourself, Writing, like reading, is second-hand living.

But do beware fact-finding/restless/creative gallivanting. Charles Dickens, for instance, would walk for miles around London, watching and listening; making notes as he did so and researching new stories. Short-circuit any such tendencies in your non-publishing quest.

goals

Don't set any goals. Graham Greene wrote 500 words a day; bollocks to that. Conrad wrote 800. More fool him. Just meander around dreamily; tell yourself you'll get around to it one day, but don't.

Google

Make sure you use Google to translate your novel into English. It will be generally incomprehensible.

The one man had touched her soul. Such vain man who can melt ice-queen facade and turns it into an avid animal, she needs his regard. Also the only one able to stop him. Because it was remaining copies of degrading video. It would destroy her if they ever drove the paparazzi. How could never be so stupid and naive, so that you can do?

But Mr X has never cheated? All newspapers of the world has covered the preparations for the wedding. Who knows what might happen? She not talked to him because of the violent, turbulent line two New Year's Eve, then.

Use Google to do your research too (see RESEARCH).

grammar, etc.

Banish grammatical, syntactical and literary inhibition, as Jack Kerouac. But not everyone's Jack Kerouac.

happiness

Happiness writes white. It is said no one writes if they're happy; so, if you're happy, why not try it? If you're unhappy, steer clear. Agatha Christie started to write detective stories during her unhappy first marriage, and look where it got her.

ignore

Ignore any submission guidelines on the publisher's website. Just do what suits you best. If the publisher asks you not to e-mail, then e-mail. If they invite you to send in a couple of sample chapters, dispatch the entire book with knobs on, Special Delivery, so you can phone up and harangue them about exactly when you sent it, how long they've had it and when exactly they will reply.

Hand-delivery is best and most intrusive, asking at reception to see the reader and refusing to leave until someone, preferably the MD, has spoken to you or made you a cup of tea. Ignore any request for a postage-paid return envelope, but expect a reply and, again, phone up to complain when you don't get one.

illustrations

Include lots of photographs, full colour, for preference, and be sure not to clear permission to use them. If you've written a cookery or a walking book, suggest each recipe or trail be photographed. Not cost effective; clearly ideal.

inner critic

Develop your inner critic, whispering in your ear just how useless you are; so you are plagued by self-doubt and never put pen to paper.

interruptions

Make sure you are constantly interrupted. When the phone rings, answer it and get into long, unnecessary conversations with friends/family/cold callers; answer the door to the gas-meter reader/charity workers/unemployed young men selling yellow dusters/Geordie fishmongers in white coats or anyone passing who knocks; surf the internet, eBay; text; Twitter. Beware occasional interruptions, which can jolt your creativity and make it flow.

isolation

To unfocus the creative frenzy, don't cultivate a willingness to be alone and be cut off. So no decamping to the woods, like Thoreau. Or retreating to a tower like Montaigne. Or getting yourself sentenced to jail like Oscar Wilde.

italics

Use random italics for emphasis, so you make the point that you have *no* confidence *at all* that anyone understands *even one single word* of what you are saying. And that you *are* writing with *great feeling BUT JUST NOT EXPRESSING YOURSELF in words*.

'I am an *Oxbridge-educated* (DPhil) (PhD) classics professor . . . here is my *real life* story, based on *true events. This is a novel . . .*'

jottings

Instead of working out a proper book plan, just jot down your ideas on the back of an envelope. Well, maybe not literally.

But in that spirit. Call up the publisher and ask them to help you get your jottings into book shape.

kudos

Glory, fame, renown, celebrity. Don't emphasize your standing, stature, esteem or reputation. Hide your light under a bushel. Celebrity? Who needs it?

length

How short is short? The Science Fiction and Fantasy Writers of America Nebula Awards for science fiction define the novel becoming a novella when the word count falls beneath 40,000 (but not below 17,500).

I have written fourteen books so far ranging from 1000 words to 20,000, but most fall into the 10,000 category . . .

Hmm, word count as a category . . . A proposal for 1000-word book or even 10,000 words is not quite book-size. Generally, bigger is better, but not too big (see EPIC). Although sometimes very short books do very well, such as Colm Tóibín's *The Testament of Mary*, which, at 30,000 words and 104 pages, can be read in an afternoon. Man Booker judges, who short listed it for the £50,000 prize, considered it unquestionably a novel; in any case, in 2013, it became the most slender work to be Booker short listed.

letter

Why bother? Just e-mail your idea, saying Hi! Or ignoring any form of address. Then paste in all your chapters. Make sure you do blind cc so publishers can see how hard you are [not] trying with your scattergun approach; that you haven't thought at all about hand-picking or selecting them specially because you like their track record in a particular genre, their successful publishing programme and expertise. Very off-putting. Ideal.

libel

Pay no attention to what might be a problem, legally. Freedom of expression. Freedom of the press. Write libellously about anyone and anything you like.

living

The well of experience that you share with everyone else; relationships and involvement with others and the world that feed your work. No! To hell with all that. Just watch lots of TV and surf the internet endlessly; drink yourself into oblivion – well, watch out for that, because it worked for Dylan Thomas.

me

Don't write for yourself; write for other people – second-guess what they might want. You can be sure they won't . . .

mildew, etc.

Consign your magnum opus to a bottom drawer in the dampest part of your home, garage or garden shed for as many years as you have, then remove it with care, add a covering letter and a few stamps to the envelope, preferably unfranked ones steamed off a used envelope, and send it off to a publisher. Don't worry that you might perchance receive a positive response – the lingering smell of mildew always sends the right message.

If you can't be bothered to wait for the mildew effect, you could try smoking as you write. If you don't smoke, find someone who does and ask them to puff away as they read. Cigar smoke's best.

Coffee- or tea-cup rings and wine-glass circles dotted over the typescript here and there, especially at the start, work well too. Mustard, Marmite or gravy stains on the cover letter are good. Or chocolatey fingerprints. Of course, there is always the Sammy Looker fishpaste option.

money

I've posted you a copy of my book by courier. E-mail me on receipt so I can sent you instructions when you can sent the money to me. Thank You

Claim this, from the outset, as your priority. Be upfront about your desire to make a shedload of money. But send in an idea that couldn't possibly make any.

niche

Make it niche, marginal, specialist; so obscure, so personal that no one has any interest in your chosen subject except you (and maybe your mum and dad). Instead of writing a book, try shooting yourself in the foot.

nuisance

Be one! Find out the name of the publisher's reader and phone them each day, first to make sure your proposal has arrived; then to see if they have read it; then to ask for a decision. A week or so later, e-mail to say that, even though they have advised you that they are having it read and considered by a commissioning editor, whose job is to buy new work, you are rewriting it and you will re-send the entire proposal again in a month or so; repeat.

If the reader is not in the office on the day you phone, ask to speak to someone else about your proposal; so they will e-mail the reader, too, to pass on the message that you phoned and are trying to get in touch. Repeat ad infinitum. No one wants an author who adds to their problems (unless they are a bestselling one); rejection is assured.

obscure

Write about something so obscure that it only ever comes up as a footnote. But beware. Sometimes even footnotes hold untapped treasures, as Roy Moxham discovered when he read a footnote about a 1500-mile hedge in India that became the starting-point for his subsequently bestselling book.

originals

Dispatch the one and only copy of your book. Do send it via regular second-class post – that way Royal Mail might do the job and lose it for you.

After a month or so, phone up the reader and say that you haven't heard back; then, when they claim no knowledge of it, accuse them of having lost it; that it took you years to write. Try everything to make that sink in: copious tears, stony silences, angry talk and dire threats; then leave them worrying on your behalf. Go ominously quiet for a couple of weeks, while the reader searches high and low for your work and builds up a backlog of unread proposals. When the reader phones to offer condolences/apologies/concern at not having found your book, say that your gardener, whom you had asked to post it, had no memory of having done so; when you had another look, you found it sitting, unsent, in a Jiffy bag beside the dog biscuits in the laundry room.

paper & pencil

Hand-write your entire submission in pencil on lined paper torn from an old exercise book. Write on both sides of the paper. When you are finished, if your last page isn't fully used, tear off the unused paper and save it for another time; carefully Sellotape a cover letter or use a hole punch to enable you to bundle it together with string. This will communicate how up to date you are on so many levels.

postage

Given that you want to keep down your costs, because not getting published takes time and money, don't use the correct postage for your submission parcel. This way the publisher will have to make up the difference, plus an extra fee, on delivery. Build on this by adding a line in your covering letter to say that you have included return postage, but of course you haven't. When you call the reader to chase your submission and they tell you they are not able to return your work without a SAE, refer them to your letter. If they don't cave in, just agree to send a SAE then don't; phone them a week or so later asking where your proposal is. To finesse this, say you've sent cash, and accuse them of pocketing it if they say they haven't received it.

prams

Larkin cautioned against the pram in the hall as a block to the writer's creativity. But, NB: times have changed.

punctuation

Don't use it. What a waste of time. Lynne Truss pedants, eat your heart out. Simply type free flow without looking at what you are typing and no checking through afterwards to see you've made sense; just like writing a text but more so.

But caution is required here. American poet e e cummings experimented with structure, form, punctuation, spelling and syntax, abandoning conventional techniques. His pared-down, playful language was so popular that, on his death, in 1962, he was the most widely read poet in the US, after Robert Frost. So watch out for that.

pushy

Don't be. Never get your elbows out and push your way to the front of the queue. Unless you want to be like Jeffrey Archer – successful, yes; someone reportedly unwilling to speak to junior staff when the MD would do.

quirky

Be as quirky as you wish. Express yourself. Channel your inner idiosyncrasies, because wacky and weird is not always wonderful. For example, arrange £3 postage in 1p stamps in a circle around the address on the return envelope – one look at this will tell anyone all they need to know about the wannabe author. And it's not a good look.

quit

Give up as soon as the first rejection letter arrives. Shout, storm, sulk, take to your bed, then go to the bottom of the garden and eat worms. Become a worm. A bookworm. Never write another word ever again, because the world doesn't deserve you. But in any case don't think about the numerous rejection letters many authors receive before they eventually get published.

read back

Beryl Bainbridge would read aloud to herself to listen to and perfect 'the music of the prose'. She edited her work all the time, cutting, distilling; ensuring not a word was wasted. Avoid doing any of this.

red font

Type your proposal in red-coloured font. Whatever point you're making, you've made it. But, consider this: perhaps it's the quality of the writing that needs to stand out?

research

Be sure not to do any research into who might be the best publisher for your book. If you've written a children's book or a fast-paced action thriller, an anthology of verse, a book of cloud clusters or an illustrated natural history of pansies, send it off to each and every one of the publishers that don't publish those sorts of books. You can rest assured that they will just send it back to you with a polite no. Repeat whenever you feel the need for a bit more rejection, disappointment and frustration.

Do no research either for the book itself. Just find everything you need via the internet and cross all your fingers and toes.

ritual & routine

No, no, no. This would be the death knell to your how-not-to-get-published scheme. Successful writers sometimes share their tricks of the trade, such as Will Self's aforementioned inner sergeant major, or Deborah Moggach's belief that she writes best in the mornings, and William Boyd's preference for writing between lunch and the cocktail hour. Never mind Jackie Collins, in a league of her own when it comes to the two Rs. Even in the days when, married to night-club owner Oscar Lerman, she would be out till 3 a.m., she was a hands-on mother, aware of bedtimes, mealtimes and up for the school run, after which she would write all day. This is an approach that has contributed to Collins' status as one of the world's top-selling novelists, with in excess of 500 million copies sold in more than forty countries, and some twenty-nine *New York Times* bestsellers to date. Don't emulate any of this, whatever you do.

skip

Avoid Elmore Leonard's advice and include the bits that readers are likely to skip. Sometimes these will be your favourite bits, which often need to come out, but, in your pursuit of failure, give yourself carte blanche to leave them in. Indeed, think of Elmore Leonard, a writer's writer, who mastered whatever genre in which he wrote. Think: What would Elmore Leonard do; then don't.

spelling

STOP! Make sure your proposal doesn't ever get Spell Checked, not even accidentally. Take pride in your unique spelling abilities that no one else can decipher except you. If anyone gives you the Lernstift pen, for your birthday perhaps, don't miss a beat: donate it directly to Oxfam or your favourite charity shop. See also Punctuation.

splinter of ice

For Graham Greene, there was a splinter of ice in the heart of a writer. Get that melted for a start.

target

As in target market or potential readers: who will buy your book? Just remember to be as vague and unfocused about this as you are able, as in, for example, 'This will appeal to everyone.' Or 'my audience is no one in particular, just anyone basically intelligent.' That's so wonderfully unhelpful that, faced with your authorial indifference to market forces, the publisher will likely struggle to find a market for your book and give up.

TV

There was no TV in the Dan Brown household when he was a child; he grew up surrounded by books and read voraciously. Plan B: watch wall-to-wall TV and banish all books from sight (except this one).

Twitter

See FACEBOOK. Refuse to engage. Say Twitter's for the birds. You'll never be one or fly high. However, once established as a writer, things are different; options unfold and allow your writing to do the talking, enabling you to avoid Twitter, if you wish.

typing

Develop Repetitive Strain Injury so you are no longer able to type. Refuse all help on that front.

unfashionable

Find a topic that is devilishly difficult to sell or out of favour from over-exposure, such as a slim volume of short stories if you're entirely unpublished, a long, academic biography of the wife of someone no one's ever heard of, a what-I-did-on-my-gap/retirement-year memoir, a treatise on the traditional Western (such as those at their fashion peak in the 1960s) or the equivalent of a bestselling misery memoir – so last year. Put together a book proposal with one of these topics in mind.

Be careful, though, like Renaissance puff pants, spats, shoulder pads, bell bottoms or knotted handkerchiefs as sun hats, your idea might be so out of time that it becomes cool and desirable again. Look what happened when Liam Gallagher and David Bowie started wearing Hush Puppies; when Burberry's Haymarket check became cool again – and again; when Cath Kidson became the new Laura Ashley. Then you might find yourself a trendsetter, as the sun rises on your proposal, the bestselling successor to Nordic Noir. Who'd have thought Scandi crime would thrive internationally? Difficult to gauge, so use with some caution or you might find yourself with a deal.

vanity

Include your favourite passport-sized photo, attach it to the cover letter in the determined belief that what you look like counts more than the quality of your work. Make sure you stress how fabulous you are; how you had a nose job, face lift, boob work; how great you'll be on TV. In any case, ensure that the content of your submission is pointless – what I did on my gap year/grey gap year, etc. usually works, unless, for instance, unfortunately, you were captured by pirates.

waffle

That cover letter – make sure it is a very long one that goes on for pages, around the houses, all the ones you have ever lived in, before getting to the point on page 66. Publishers get so many submissions that it's not likely they will pursue what looks unlikely from the start. Keep the focus off the book and keep it wordy and irrelevant. You'll soon lose everyone amid the verbose preamble; so they won't ever find your gem of an idea lurking a long way towards the back.

X-factor

Simply don't have one. You've seen it on TV. Don't try it on the page. Never reveal your X-factor – that unexplainable something that adds that vital je ne sais quoi. If you do, you might attract interest. Do not make the best or most of yourself under any circumstances, if you want to stay unpublished.

Of course, literary history is littered with the modest, retiring or otherwise inhibited, such as Jane Austen, who wrote on small pieces of paper that were easy to slide under a desk blotter whenever someone surprised her by coming into the room as she was writing; her books were published anonymously, sometimes as A Lady. But times have changed.

yellowed paper

The typescript has yellowed with age; the pages are well thumbed and the corners torn – do not push the boat out and print afresh each time you send out your typescript, unless you want to be in the game. See also MILDEW, ETC.

zeal

On no account put any passion or zeal into what you have written. Keep it entirely vapid, vague and vacant. See also TARGET.

zzzzz

A row of Zs. Fall asleep on the couch in front of the TV and don't go near the computer or put pen to paper; don't finish that book you have been trying to write for the past decade. Do anything other than write it. Instead, talk about it endlessly at parties/in bus queues; get yourself a chaise-longue (writerly pretensions without the graft) and stretch out on it at every opportunity. Easier that way – and you can still do your party piece about that novel you intend to write.

Who'd Be a Writer Now?

Created in 1946 and named after Edgar Allen Poe, the Edgar Awards were and remain a major accolade for distinguished work in the mystery genre. The year after James Patterson's debut, The Thomas Berryman Number, *was published (1976), the Mystery Writers of America, organizers of the Edgars, got in touch to invite him to their Awards ceremony. Not expecting his refusal (due to a prior engagement), they had no alternative but to reveal that Patterson's presence was required because he would be receiving an award. Patterson heard what they said but it didn't quite register until he found himself on the podium making his acceptance speech, at which point he also felt able to say: 'I guess I'm a writer now.'*

But don't give up the day job. Patterson's career trajectory is far from typical (including the fact that, among other achievements, since 2006, he has written one out of every seventeen hardback novels bought in the US; he was the most borrowed author in UK libraries in 2013, according to data released in February 2014 by Public Lending Right – a place he has held since 2007). The Authors Licensing and Collecting Society (ALCS) is a membership organization for writers, run by its members, for its members. Key findings from an ALCS survey of 25,000 writers reveal some bleak and yet not-so-surprising results:

- Income wise, writing is a high-risk profession. *Who knew!*
- A professional author's income is typically a third less than the national average.
- The younger you are, the less you'll earn, rising in your thirties to peak in your mid-fifties then down, down again.
- Mind the gender gap – female authors earn less than their male counterparts. *No surprise there.*
- Like all the creative industries, writing's a game in which winner-takes-all: the top 10 per cent of authors earn more than 50 per cent of total income, while the bottom 50 per cent earn less than 10 per cent. *Sounds familiar . . .*

But surely the advent of self-publishing has changed things? Well, yes and no, but the fact is that it isn't such a goldmine for writers either. From figures for 2011, most DIY writers earned an average $10,000 (£6,375) – and half made less than $500 (about £300), despite the considerable splash of self-publishing successes such as Amanda Hocking and E. L. James.

The inconvenient truth is that writers' earnings are deteriorating in real terms – unless you happen to be one of those listed in *Forbes* magazine's top-earning authors. Well, that is something to aim for, perhaps; but it is hardly a surprise to see that E. L. James heads up the *Forbes* list for 2012–13, expanded here to include some of its stellar authors' top writing tips and inspirations.

E. L. James: $95 million

An early version of the *Fifty Shades* trilogy began as Twilight fan fiction posted on the internet. The books were found there by The Writer's Coffee Shop, an Australian publisher, which released the trilogy as ebooks and print-on-demand paperbacks. The ebook is key to the James phenomenon, ensuring the steamy read that is *Fifty Shades* is easy to buy and read discreetly in public. It launched James into the stratosphere, atop every bestseller list. James's advice for aspiring writers is to write for oneself; to stop thinking about writing and just do it; put words to paper as an inspiration to continue.

James Patterson: $91 million

Patterson typed his first novel at the kitchen table of his small New York apartment each night after work and at weekends. Some four decades later, he writes long-hand and has his books typed up by an assistant. In 2011, an estimated one in four of all hardback suspense/thriller novels sold was by Patterson; he became the first author to achieve five million ebook sales (rising, doubling, fast), and he holds the Guinness record for the most No. 1 *New York Times* bestsellers of any author. He maintains his elevated tenancy on the *Forbes* list via his adult thrillers; his Witch & Wizard and Maximum Ride series make him a bestselling young-adult author too.

Suzanne Collins: $55 million

Author of the five-book Underland Chronicles, Collins' scifi trilogy *The Hunger Games*'s adaptation into a blockbuster movie propelled her to No. 3. Collins believes that writing about what you feel passionately about makes the process easier; her advice to young writers is to write not just what they know but also what they find fascinating or exciting.

Bill O'Reilly: $28 million

The success of Fox News host O'Reilly's *Killing Lincoln* (written with historian Martin Dugard) made writing books a highly lucrative optional extra for him. The anchor of *The O'Reilly Factor*, the highest-rated cable news show in the US, he is also the author of several number-one bestselling books, including *Killing Kennedy*, which reached Nos 1 and 2 on the *New York Times* hardback non-fiction bestseller list.

Danielle Steel: $26 million

Steel's 2013 novel, *Until the End of Time*, debuted at No. 1 on the *New York Times* bestseller list. In her four decades as a published author, she has written 128 books, mostly romances, averaging more than three a year. She is published in sixty-nine countries and forty-three languages. All her books are bestsellers – with 600 million copies sold internationally.

Jeff Kinney: $24 million

Kinney was an aspiring newspaper cartoonist, who transformed himself into a bestselling children's author. In 1998 he began work on *Diary of a Wimpy Kid* and continued for six years before publishing it online in daily instalments (to date, the online version is read by more than 70,000 people a day). In 2006, he achieved a multi-book deal and the book moved into print. By 2013, it had spawned eight instalments, of which No. 7, *The Third Wheel*, sold more than 1.4 million copies in 2012.

Janet Evanovich: $24 million

Evanovich started with romance then turned to crime. On her website, she describes herself as a workaholic who motivates herself to write by spending her money before she makes it. Making money is not an issue, in some part due to the great success of her Stephanie Plum detective series. The secrets of her success are divulged in her book on writing and being an author, *How I Write*.

Nora Roberts: $23 million

Published in more than thirty countries, since her first bestseller in 1991, Roberts' books have spent 949 weeks on

Something Nasty in the Slushpile

the *New York Times* bestseller list – equivalent to more than eighteen consecutive years of weekly bestsellers. Favouring her trademark genre of popular romance, she has enjoyed success with fantasy and suspense too. By 2012, with sales of more than 3.2 million digital copies of her books (second only to E. L. James), she is a queen of the ebook.

Dan Brown: $22 million

Blockbuster Brown has said that reading legendary agent Albert Zuckerman's *Writing the Blockbuster Novel* helped him finish his first novel, *Digital Fortress*, and get it published. Brown's *Inferno*, about the adventures of occult mystery-solver Robert Langdon, was a 2013 bestseller, although sales were less strong than for its predecessors, *The Da Vinci Code* and *The Lost Symbol*.

Stephen King: $20 million

Carrie was rejected by some thirty publishers, but the book's eventual success changed everything for King, enabling him to write full time. His published output now ranks him almost on a par with Agatha Christie. He is said to write 2000 words each day and wrote *The Running Man* in a week (but was not able to sell it). He claims he has never been an intellectual writer, only ever wanting to 'scare the shit' out of his readers. With book sales of 400 million, if that's what he's doing, he's doing it right. The *New York Times* describes him as impossible to resist, a 'relentless tidal pull' that sucks you in. Many of King's books, from *Carrie* onwards, have been adapted for cinema; US box-office profits from *Carrie* total $33.8 million. Like many of the ideas for his novels, the spur for his fifty-sixth novel, *Doctor Sleep* (a sequel to *The Shining*), came from a newspaper article about a hospice cat that sensed when people were about to die and would go to their room to sleep curled up beside them.

Dean Koontz: $20 million

Dean Koontz won an *Atlantic Monthly* fiction competition when he was a college student and is now one of America's most popular suspense novelists. When he started out, writing after work, at nights and weekends, his wife offered to support him for a period of five years; if he couldn't make it as a writer in that time, he'd never make it. His books now exist in thirty-eight languages, with fourteen of his novels having hit No.1 on the *New York Times* hardback bestseller list. His book sales total more than 450 million copies to date.

John Grisham: $18 million

Grisham would get up at five in the morning to work on his first novel, *A Time to Kill*, published in 1988 after three years' writing and numerous rejections. He gave up his law career when he sold the film rights to his next book, *The Firm*, to Paramount for $600,000; book rights followed. One of what are now his trademark legal thrillers, *The Firm* was 1991's bestselling novel. He has written a novel a year since *A Time to Kill*.

David Baldacci: $15 million

Like John Grisham, Baldacci practised law before he became a career novelist. He began to write at high school. While working as a lawyer, he wrote late evening and into the early morning. His debut novel, *Absolute Power* (1996), was adapted for the screen with Clint Eastwood as its director and star. He has published twenty-six bestselling novels; his work is translated into more than forty-five languages and sold in some eighty countries.

Rick Riordan: $14 million

As an award-winning author of adult mysteries, Riordan reportedly began to write young-adult fiction after being inspired by a bedtime story he read to his son. The Percy Jackson and the Olympians series (plus the 39 Clues initiative) have brought him success; in 2012 he sold more than 5.6 million copies of his mythology-inspired YA adventures, with two out of every three bestselling children's titles Riordan's. The first book that Riordan says he remembers reading for fun was *Lord of the Rings*; at one stage he had Tolkien's map of Middle Earth stuck to his bedroom wall, which inspired him to draw his own maps of fantasy worlds. In the teaching work that preceded his writing career, he liked to make education fun, believing that, if he was enjoying himself, his pupils would enjoy it too. He senses the same is true of writing and readers.

J. K. Rowling: $13 million

Rowling has said she has the ideal temperament for a writer: content to be alone in a room, making things up. Known as Joanne Rowling when *Harry Potter* (*and the Philosopher's Stone*) was first found in the slushpile, the 'K', for Kathleen, the name of her paternal grandmother, was added at the request of her publisher, in the belief that a woman's name might be off-putting to the Harry Potter target audience of young boys. More than 450 million copies of Rowling's seven Harry Potter books have been sold world wide to date. Smoothly navigating the shift from children's books to adult fiction, *The Cuckoo's Calling* (writing as Robert Galbraith) topped the hardback bestseller lists in 2013; while her first novel for adults, *The Casual Vacancy* (2012), was first among paperbacks, with a BBC-TV adaptation scheduled for 2014. Rowling has added screenwriting to her glorious cv, with the first in a new series for Warner Bros, *Fantastic Beasts and Where to Find Them*, her debut.

George R. R. Martin: $12 million

It took Martin six years to write *A Dance with Dragons*, the most recent instalment, book five, in his magnum-opus fantasy series, *A Song of Ice and Fire*. But HBO's adaptation of the series debut, *A Game of Thrones*, a Best Book of 1996 and a *Publishers Weekly* starred review, made him the second best-selling paperback writer of 2012 (after E. L. James).

The Slushpile is Dead!
Long Live the Slushpile!

As the world of book publishing spins on a new axis, in an ongoing revolution that began with the ebook, could the slushpile's days be numbered? Or has it just been reinvented with the proliferation of online writing communities of writers, readers and publishers working together to spot new talent?

The fact is the traditional slushpile is no longer the integral part of publishing life that it once was. Increasingly, publishers are not accepting work sent to them cold, without the filter of a literary agency. And so other paths to getting published are being forged in an eternally shifting bookscape.

Take Authonomy, for example. Its website strapline declares it to be not just a community of book lovers but also the place where writers become authors; where great books get published. It builds on that with Authoright's range of book services – from editing and publishing to online and book marketing – for self-publishing authors, as well as traditionally published writers with a literary agent. There's advice too on how not to drown in the slushpile – and the website itself operates as an electronic slushpile, dedicated to flushing out then fleshing out the brightest and best. Not so much a refusal to accept unsolicited submissions then, but a different approach to them.

Bookcountry.com is another online community, where members post manuscripts and exchange feedback. The site also offers a service to design, publish and distribute ebooks. Penguin signed its first writer from Bookcountry in 2012, just a year after creating it, with the partial aim of discovering new talent. Kerry Schafer's novel, *Between*, which Penguin went on to publish, was spotted by a literary agent after Schafer had posted excerpts of it on Bookcountry.

Self-publishing opportunities abound with Amazon's KDP (Kindle Direct Publishing) and Barnes & Noble's Nook Press (launched in 2013 to replace its predecessor PubIt!). Places like Smashwords (founded in 2008 to change how books are published, marketed and sold, with the strapline: your ebook, your way). Like Amazon, Smashwords is free for authors to use. There is a burgeoning array of options available for ebook self-publishing, from Lulu and iBooks Author to CreateSpace and Booktango.

Ether Books is a mobile social-reading platform that aims to connect writers and readers around the world. They publish 'made for mobile' Quick Reads to smartphone, Facebook and Tablet users. Their USP is to discover talented new and bestselling writers; provide a social-publishing platform that works with new writers to publish short reads. Authors submit work direct to them, registering first then creating an Ether profile and submitting work for consideration. Ether curate all the work that they publish so only what they deem the pick of the crop is released on to their platform, with their published writers gaining access to the Ether community.

Yet another way to turn your big book idea into a financed reality is online crowdfunding. Anyone looking to crowdfund a book and assess the potential of a book idea might consider Pubslush, which describes itself as a global, crowdfunded publishing platform with a cause.

And so on …

With such a range of diverse initiatives popping up like daisies after spring rain, the publishing revolution is well under way, taking the slushpile along with it. Perhaps everyone's a slushpile reader now.